Gorbachev's "New Thinking" on Terrorism

THE WASHINGTON PAPERS

. . . intended to meet the need for an authoritative, yet prompt, public appraisal of the major developments in world affairs.

President, CSIS: David M. Abshire

Series Editor: Walter Laqueur

Director of Publications: Nancy B. Eddy

Managing Editor: Donna R. Spitler

MANUSCRIPT SUBMISSION

The Washington Papers and Praeger Publishers welcome inquiries concerning manuscript submissions. Please include with your inquiry a curriculum vitae, synopsis, table of contents, and estimated manuscript length. Manuscripts must be between 120–200 double-spaced typed pages. All submissions will be peer reviewed. Submissions to *The Washington Papers* should be sent to *The Washington Papers*; The Center for Strategic and International Studies; 1800 K Street NW; Suite 400; Washington, DC 20006. Book proposals should be sent to Praeger Publishers; One Madison Avenue; New York NY 10010.

The Washington Papers/141

Gorbachev's "New Thinking" on Terrorism

Galia Golan

Foreword by Walter Laqueur

Published with The Center for
Strategic and International Studies
Washington, D.C.

New York
Westport, Connecticut
London

Library of Congress Cataloging-in-Publication Data

Golan, Galia.
  Gorbachev's "new thinking" on terrorism / Galia Golan.
    p. cm. — (The Washington papers, ISSN 0278-937X ; 141)
  "Published with the Center for Strategic and International
Studies, Washington, D.C."
  Includes bibliographical references.
  ISBN 0-275-93482-9 (alk. paper). — ISBN 0-275-93483-7 (pbk. :
alk. paper)
  1. Terrorism—Government policy—Soviet Union. I. Center
for Strategic and International Studies.
II. Title. III. Series.
HV6433.S65G65   1990
363.3′2′0947—dc20   89-23039

The *Washington Papers* are written under the auspices of The Center
for Strategic and International Studies (CSIS) and published
with CSIS by Praeger Publishers. The views expressed in these papers
are those of the authors and not necessarily those of the Center.

Library of Congress Catalog Card Number: 89-23039
ISBN: 0-275-93482-9 (cloth)
        0-275-93483-7 (paper)

First published in 1990

Praeger Publishers, One Madison Avenue, New York, NY 10010
A division of Greenwood Press, Inc.

Printed in the United States of America

∞

The paper used in this book complies with the
Permanent Paper Standard issued by the National
Information Standards Organization (Z39.48-1984).

10 9 8 7 6 5 4 3 2 1

Contents

Foreword

Marxist-Leninist theory has always been critical of the individual use of terrorism. It believed in revolution, and revolutions were carried out by classes, not individual plotters. It involved the long, arduous work of organization and propaganda, and those who believed that throwing a few bombs would change history were deeply mistaken. As Trotsky once noted: "The classes whom the state serves will always find new men—the mechanism remains intact and continues to function." But Marx, Engels, and Lenin did not reject terrorism as a matter of moral principle; in certain conditions they thought it might work. Thus Marx supported (within limits) the Irish Fenians and for a while also the *Narodnaia Volia*, the Russian terrorists of the 1870s and 1880s. Broadly speaking, Lenin's attitude was similar, but it is only fair to add that his emphasis was always on collective rather than individual action.

The Soviet attitude toward terrorism during the 1960s and 1970s was also negative, but there were so many exceptions to the rule that outside observers were bound to become confused. The Soviet leaders certainly opposed right-wing terrorism and had their misgivings about the terrorism of the extreme left. But they thought that terrorism was legitimate when applied by national liberation movements, at least if it was directed against the Western powers. This support was not purely platonic; military, financial, and logistical help was rendered, admittedly more often through satellites because it was deemed unseemly for a superpower to be caught in the act of giving direct assistance.

Since about 1983–1984 – that is, even before the advent of Gorbachev – there has been a hardening of the Soviet line toward terrorism, at least on the ideological level. Viktor Vitiuk's *Leftist Terrorism*, to which Galia Golan's study refers, gave a fairly realistic account of why terrorism had developed in certain countries and what could be done about it. The no-nonsense approach contrasted with the writings of certain Western writers who continued to believe that one man's terrorist was another man's freedom fighter.

To what extent has Soviet practice been matched by such ideological insights? It is difficult to answer this with total certainty. It is certainly true that Soviet observers have concluded that terrorism causes more harm than good and could be a major stumbling block on the road toward improving relations with the West. Furthermore, there was a gradual understanding that although in the past there had been little, if any, terrorism against Soviet objects, the situation may not always remain thus; the Soviet Union could therefore benefit – up to a point – from international cooperation against terrorism.

On the other hand, not all support for national liberation movements could be dropped, and Soviet relations with Qadhafi (defined as a "comrade" in the Soviet media), as well as with Iran and Syria, remained close. It could always be argued that they (the Russians) were not their brothers' keepers, but in the real world of international politics this argument does not carry much weight. Thus, the Soviet Union still faces a dilemma, not so much in its attitude toward terrorism but in its relations with its friends' friends. Professor Golan has long been one of the most careful students of this dilemma in Soviet policy, and her new study represents the most penetrating analysis to date of how the new Soviet leadership views the problem of terrorism.

Walter Laqueur
Chairman, International Research Council
Center for Strategic and International Studies

September 1989

About the Author

Galia Golan is the Jay and Leoni Darwin Professor of Soviet and East European Studies and chairperson of the Department of Political Science at the Hebrew University of Jerusalem. She is also former director of the Mayrock Center for Soviet and East European Research at the Hebrew University. Educated at Brandeis University, l'École Pratique des Hautes Études in Paris, and the Hebrew University, she is the author of five books: *The Soviet Union and National Liberation Movements in the Third World* (1988); *The Soviet Union and the Palestine Liberation Organization: An Uneasy Alliance* (1980); *Yom Kippur and After: The Soviet Union and the Middle East Crisis* (1977); *Reform Rule in Czechoslovakia: The Dubcek Era* (1973); *The Czechoslovak Reform Movement: Communism in Crisis 1962-1968* (1971); and *Soviet Policies in the Middle East since World War Two* (forthcoming).

Acknowledgment

Over the past two years, the Center for Strategic and International Studies has conducted a study of Soviet policy toward the Third World under Mikhail Gorbachev. The Soviet studies program of CSIS is pleased to acknowledge the generous support for this effort provided by the J. Howard Pew Freedom Trust.

Among the publications of this project are three Washington Papers, including the current work by Galia Golan of the Hebrew University. The first in the series, *Gorbachev's Military Policy in the Third World*, by Mark Katz of George Mason University, was published earlier in 1989. The concluding volume is *Gorbachev's Economic Strategy in the Third World*, by Giovanni Graziani of the University of Padua (forthcoming).

Stephen Sestanovich
Director of Soviet Studies
Center for Strategic
and International Studies
Washington, D.C.

Summary

The reevaluation of Soviet foreign policy under Mikhail Gorbachev — the "new thinking" — has produced a new Soviet attitude and apparently a different behavior toward terrorism. In the past, terrorism was officially condemned either as a method used by imperialist or capitalist regimes against an oppressed population or as an illegitimate offshoot of armed struggle that has nothing in common with genuine liberation struggles. Under Gorbachev, terrorism has been clearly categorized under regional conflicts, with the admission (usually only implicit) that national liberation and revolutionary groups have been using this method.

Identifying terrorism in the category of regional conflicts subjects terrorism to the new rules of regional conflict. Under "new thinking," these rules call for the peaceful resolution of such conflicts through political means only. If armed struggle for progressive causes (national liberation, socialist revolution) used to be acceptable in some form as a supplement to political methods, today military means of any kind are ruled out altogether. The past, usually arbitrary, public Soviet distinction between the legitimate use of force by national liberation movements (sometimes called "revolutionary violence") on the one hand and terrorism on the other hand has given way to condemnation of the use of force, including terrorism, however and by whomever it is used.

Gorbachev's Defense Minister D. T. Yazov accepted this rejection of force as part of the new Soviet defensive military doctrine and espoused it for the resolution of conflicts abroad. But a number of military researchers and theoreticians concerned in the past with issues of local wars and Third World struggles were decidedly more conservative. Citing Lenin on the existence of just wars, they termed the new policy "pacifism" and defended the right of national liberation movements to employ all means, including armed struggle. It was this group that persisted in distinguishing between terrorism, which they had always condemned, and what they called the legitimate use of force in the struggle for liberation. From mid-1987, however, this criticism diminished, and few were the comments opposing the new position.

The new attitude has been accompanied by a new cooperative approach to international terrorism. The Soviets have proposed bilateral cooperation with individual Western countries in talks with various leaders and have proposed an international conference on combating terrorism as well. Moscow has sought to be included in Western meetings on the subject and in January 1989 hosted an unofficial conference by a U.S.-Soviet task force of experts who agreed to produce a joint study, including recommendations to their respective governments, on terrorism. A top KGB official publicly expressed his willingness to cooperate with British, U.S., and Israeli intelligence, following Soviet-Israeli cooperation in handling a terrorist incident in December 1988. And Soviet and East European officials reportedly have provided the West with some intelligence information on known terrorists and occasionally have taken action against the facilities and operatives of Libya and of the Abu Nidal group working inside the Soviet bloc.

The issue of Soviet arms supplies to groups using terrorism has been raised only indirectly and most tentatively within the Soviet Union. It is by no means clear if any change has taken place in actual arms deliveries or other aid, such as training and logistics, rendered these groups in the past. In the past two years, there has been a decline in the number of terrorist incidents conducted by most of the Moscow-supported groups. And the message from Moscow to such groups as the Palestine Liberation Organization and the African National Congress has clearly called for the abandonment of armed struggle (including terrorism) in favor of political solutions. The negotiations that have been opened in a large number of ongoing conflicts, even those of the Polisario in the western Sahara and the Basques in Spain, may be connected with this message and possibly with some change in the concrete assistance these movements may now expect to receive from Moscow.

Despite what appears to be a reduction in Soviet aid to many groups using terrorism, there have been reports and rumors of new Soviet involvement—in the Philippines and Pakistan, for example. Involvement in the Philippines is far from clear, but there was a sharp increase in terrorist acts perpetrated by the Soviet-supported Afghan intelligence service operating in Pakistan. Despite speculation that these acts were conducted independently of Moscow or at least of the orders connected with the "new thinking," it appears more likely that they were an attempt to pressure the Pakistani government to abandon support for the rebel struggle in Afghanistan as Moscow implemented its withdrawal. Only time will tell if this was an exception to the new policy or proof that there is no new policy in the field. The appointment of a new head of the KGB in Moscow, a man long associated with Gorbachev's mentor Yuri Andropov, suggests that this institution, which shares responsibility with military intelligence for Soviet involvement with groups employing terrorism, will more closely follow the "new thinking" in the future.

The Soviet approach to terrorism against its own targets—that is, against Soviet personnel in the Soviet Union and Eastern Europe, or against regimes supported by them—

Introduction

Soviet attitudes and policies toward terrorism have never been easy to determine. Official rhetoric has always been subject to ideological and practical considerations as well as to propaganda interests. Designed to respond to accusations, be they from suspicious enemies or wary allies, public Soviet statements have never provided more than partial, often contradictory, evidence regarding actual positions. Given the nature of the phenomenon of terrorism itself, Soviet policies and behavior behind the rhetoric have generally been closed to outside scrutiny. Only rarely, and often with dubious authenticity, have pieces of information surfaced to provide some clues to Soviet attitudes. And the actual role played by the Soviet Union in its relations with

I thank my research assistants Brenda Sheffer and Alek Milman, whose intelligent and dedicated help has been invaluable to me. And I thank the Hebrew University of Jerusalem's Mayrock Center for Soviet and East European Research and Truman Institute, as well as the Jaffee Center for Strategic Studies of Tel Aviv University and the Rand Corporation, for the use of their documentation and research facilities. I am also grateful to the Van Leer Institute of Jerusalem for the lovely surroundings in which to write. – G. G.

1

groups using terrorism has often been the subject of speculation, even fantasy, rather than verifiable research.

The advent of greater Soviet openness, in foreign as
well as domestic matters, has done little to alter these basic
difficulties in obtaining information. Terrorism, almost by
definition, is not a topic on which one might expect to find a
great deal of public debate, or openly admitted, publicized
policy changes, even in the era of *glasnost* (openness). As
was the case before Mikhail Gorbachev, one can only begin
to build a picture from public Soviet comments on the phenomenon of terrorism in general (usually directed toward —
and against — the West) and by extrapolating from discussions of such broader subjects as armed struggle and
methods of liberation. Aside from evidence produced by
non-Soviet sources, occasionally from the very groups that
employ terrorism, there is today a small but growing body
of evidence on actual steps taken by Moscow in coordination with Western governments or international organizations. This in itself indicates a change in the Soviet approach toward terrorism under the "new thinking" of Soviet
foreign policy.

New thinking is the foreign policy counterpart of the
domestic *perestroika* (restructuring). Prompted by what
has been termed the "stagnation" in Soviet foreign policy
under Leonid Brezhnev, new thinking has been designed to
redefine the place and role of the Soviet Union in the world
today. Yet new thinking is not a complete or fully formed
theory; it is not even a clearly delineated set of ideas. In
a sense it is still at the stage of a theory in the making,
including a process of retrospective and innovative exami-
nation of the basic concepts governing Soviet foreign policy.
Certain aspects have taken form, and concepts such as "interdependence" of states and the need to proceed according
to a "balance of interests" in world affairs have been promulgated, along with the dictum to take ideology out of
foreign relations. A number of areas and concepts, however,
are still being reevaluated. Some of them are directly relevant or essential to the issue of terrorism. Thus, the general

attitude toward national liberation movements, their function in international as well as Soviet policies, and the related issue of armed struggle appear to be in the as yet "unfinished" category.

Given this substantive limitation as well as the methodological problems involved, it is nonetheless possible to make a preliminary analysis of the changes that have taken place within the framework of new thinking. A good deal of discussion has occurred, as well as some action at the international level and signals to various groups engaged in terrorism—all of which indicate Gorbachev's developing attitude and his regime's policies toward terrorism.

1

Background: The Soviet Attitude toward Terrorism

Since prerevolutionary days, terrorism as a method has received little or no support from official Soviet ideology. The early Bolsheviks at most were ambivalent to such action. Indeed, one of the distinguishing factors between the Russian Social Democrats (both Bolsheviks and Mensheviks) and the Social Revolutionaries was the latter's support for the use of terrorism. The Bolsheviks explicitly condemned the use of terrorism by both the Social Revolutionaries and the Narodnaia Volya (nineteenth-century revolutionary group). Although Lenin characterized this Bolshevik opposition to terrorism as a position of expediency, he himself warned against indiscriminate terrorism.[1] Later Soviet theoreticians expressed this position in the words of Lenin: "Propagation of terror as a means of the revolutionary awakening of the masses represents worship of spontaneity by the intelligentsia, which has no connection with the revolutionary work of the workers' movement."[2]

Such "revolutionary work" was primarily organizational and educational activity directed toward coordinated mass action that would be determined by concrete as well as historical socioeconomic circumstances. This action, which might or might not include violence, would have nothing in common with the indiscriminate or individual

5

violence defined as terrorism. The type of violence envisioned by Lenin always depended upon historical and social circumstances. It involved civil (class) warfare rather than guerrilla warfare, sabotage rather than terrorism—that is, an organized, systematic action by the masses dictated by objective social forces and structures, rather than spontaneous, sporadic individual action dictated by emotional (in Marxist-Leninist terminology, "subjectivist") outbursts and utopian "voluntarism."[3]

Postrevolutionary Soviet policy differed little from these early positions. The issue of violence as a revolutionary tactic still received more attention than terrorism. Nikita Khrushchev's policy of peaceful coexistence and a peaceful road to socialism was prompted among other things by a perception of greater risk in the era of nuclear weapons, and Soviet ideology increasingly challenged the use of force as a revolutionary tactic. Although by no means a blanket rejection, general Soviet opposition to revolutionary violence and the use of force, nevertheless, became a central issue in the Sino-Soviet conflict. The Soviet position condemned what it called the Chinese belief in "revolution through the barrel of a gun." These polemics and discussions, however, dealt only rarely with the issue of terrorism.[4]

Official definitions of terrorism under Brezhnev focused on the type of terrorism used by regimes or rulers to sustain their rule, impose their will, and suppress opposition. References were limited to capitalist, right-wing, or fascist regimes, to imperialist or occupying forces, or to Maoist China. As a method to be used by those holding the reins of power, this type of terrorism fell into a loose category of "state terrorism," from which socialist states were, by definition, excluded (except for the brief period of socialist construction when "revolutionary terror" against "militarized" internal opponents was legitimate).[5] Singled out in this loose category of state or regime terrorism was not only Maoist China (accused, for example, of employing terrorism through Pol Pot when he was in power), but also such "neofascist" or "neocolonialist" regimes as South Africa, southern Rhodesia, or Israel. After the early Reagan administration accused Moscow of being at the center of modern international terrorism, Soviet emphasis on terrorism as an instrument of capitalist states — especially the United States or its allies — became a very popular theme. Much less frequent were references to terrorism as a method used by groups or individuals that were seeking power or operating against established regimes or state interests. This type of terrorism was subjected to a different set of considerations and analytical criteria.[6]

Military versus Political Means

The method of terrorism used by those out of power — by national liberation or revolutionary movements, for example — was understood as one of several types of armed struggle. As such, it had to be evaluated within the framework of armed versus peaceful (political) means before it could be compared with other forms of armed struggle. Even during the Brezhnev period, there was a variety of views on this basic issue of armed versus peaceful means, suggesting ambivalence, possibly even disagreement, within the Soviet foreign policy elite.

Overall, academic, party, and even military opinion favored political over military means. Because leadership pronouncements were rare, much of this opinion was apparent from indirect rather than direct references. Although armed struggle was not ruled out, a number of arguments were used to clarify preferences. Many used Leninist admonitions against "putschism" or adventurism to oppose the precipitous use, if any, of force. Both revolutionary and mass-based movements required that priority be given to political, organizational, and ideological work — that is, peaceful means.

Some saw a complementary role for armed action; indeed, few actually rejected the use of force out of hand, preferring rather to subordinate it nearly to the point of discounting its efficacy and its necessity. They were particularly concerned with the challenge offered by violence-centered theories popular among some national liberation or radical revolutionary movements—for example, the ideas of Franz Fanon and Mao Zedong. According to such party theorists as A. I. Sobolev, then deputy head of the Institute for Marxism-Leninism of the Central Committee's Ideology Department, their ideas challenged the Soviet view of Marxist-Leninist revolutionary doctrine and also introduced such non-Soviet features as spontaneity and a preference for the countryside.[7]

Much opposition, however, was influenced also by a more pragmatic interest in détente and the prevention of conflict, including a concern about the escalation of local wars. Condemnation of armed struggle, even in the criticism of Chinese doctrine, was often couched in détente-related terms. Similarly, détente itself was invoked by these opponents of force as a factor that reduced, if not eliminated, the need for armed struggle. Adherents to this position included the deputy head of the Central Committee's International Department Karen Brutents, and even his more conservative superior Rostislav Ul'ianovskii, as well as then head of the Oriental Institute Evgenii Primakov.

Nonetheless, a number of theoreticians explicitly supported the idea of armed struggle. Most, like Gleb Starushenko, deputy head of the Africa Institute, saw it as a simple matter of defending the right to use this form of struggle. But some saw armed struggle as an inevitable, integral, even essential part of the revolutionary or liberation struggle. They, like S. L. Agaev of the Institute for the International Workers' Movement, became more vocal in response to the fall of Chilean President Salvador Allende in 1973 and again a few years later with the successful revolution in Nicaragua.[8] Those accepting, possibly even advocating, the use of force argued for the "divisibility of détente": Détente applied to relations between states but in no way limited the revolutionary or national liberation struggle. This argument ignored any damage such tactics might cause détente, suggesting that opposition to détente itself may have motivated these advocates of force.

The military fueled this position by categorizing wars of national liberation as "just" wars rather than as local wars (the latter were by definition subject to escalation) or by eliminating the concept of inevitable escalation as applied to local wars. Military writers, by no means uniform in their appraisal of local wars and the possibility of escalation, held somewhat different views about the inevitability as well as desirability of armed struggle. As a more sophisticated (that is, differentiated) approach to local wars was developed in the 1970s, notably by head of the General Staff Academy General I. Shavrov, wars of national liberation—the form of armed struggle most widely accepted—became more problematic for these theorists. Yet as the estimate about the escalation of local conflict itself became more varied, such wars could more easily be accepted. The military leadership leaned toward the older concern about the inevitability of escalation, possibly preferring stability to the risk of involvement in armed conflict, but even leadership pronouncements among the military were not unequivocal.

The same may be said about the civilian leadership of the Soviet Union. Avoiding any explicit expression of preferences regarding means, some leaders such as Yuri Andropov and Alexei Kosygin did speak of the people's right to fight for independence "guns in hand." Brezhnev, Andrei Gromyko, and ideology watchdog Mikhail Suslov used the idea of divided détente to accommodate this struggle, and Boris Ponomarev appeared actually to favor recourse to arms. Andropov qualified his position with frequent warnings about the risks of escalation and instability, while Brezhnev refrained from clear support, even at the peak of his enthusiasm for Third World states and movements at the 1976 Congress of the Communist Party of the Soviet Union (CPSU). By the 1981 CPSU Congress and particularly in the last year of his life, Brezhnev retreated from this support, emphasizing a need for stability and a concern about escalation, even as he acknowledged the variety of means used by revolutionaries, including armed struggle. Nikolai Podgornyi, also acknowledging the use of armed means, explicitly declared Moscow's preference for political means during his 1977 trip to Africa.

Types of Armed Struggle

A Soviet typology of armed struggle may be discerned from published Soviet sources on the subject, albeit a very small body of work. This typology consists of sabotage (defined in the West as violence against property), terrorism (violence against civilians), guerrilla warfare (irregular military action against military targets), and conventional warfare (civil war or wars of national liberation fought by regular units). Practically speaking, this typology appeared to be viewed as a continuum, from sabotage to guerrilla warfare to conventional warfare, with terrorism as an offshoot of guerrilla warfare or sabotage. In such a continuum, guerrilla war might precede, even prepare the ground for, conventional warfare, but it was nonetheless subordinate to it.

One study declared the struggles in Yugoslavia, China, and Vietnam to be massive guerrilla wars, adding that they had developed into "the activity of regular national liberation armies."[9] Vietnam, for example, was cited as a model, with a first stage of political propaganda, leadership training, and the creation of legal and underground resistance organizations; its second stage consisted of guerrilla struggle with organized insurgency bases; and its third stage involved the expansion of large-scale guerrilla war into a regular war of mobility, including the use of attacks or military formations, regular armed forces (divisions, regiments, battalions, companies), and, for auxiliary tasks, paramilitary forces such as guerrilla units and people's militia. Latin American revolutionary leader Che Guevara was even quoted to the effect that "guerrilla war is only a stage of regular war and, therefore, guerrilla struggle alone cannot achieve final victory." As the Soviet study added, "Only the transformation of guerrilla units into units of a regular type and dealing crushing blows to government troops are capable of securing the final victory for the insurgents."[10]

Why was conventional warfare preferred over guerrilla warfare? The issue involved not only stages in a continuum but also the issue of setting – the countryside versus the city. Guerrilla warfare was a struggle conducted in the countryside, by peasants. Given the Marxist-Leninist preference for the city and for workers – distinct from the dubious revolutionary potential and level of the peasantry – an identification of guerrilla warfare with the rural areas rendered it suspect. Moreover, the city was deemed the central bastion of power – governmental, economic, and military – and as such the focal point for the decisive final battle.

As was the case with the issue of armed versus political struggle, some dissenting voices expressed interest in, and even preferred, guerrilla warfare.[11] Specifically after the success of revolutionary guerrilla forces in Nicaragua, commentators in the Soviet journal *Latinskaia Amerika* suggested that the Soviet opposition to this form of struggle be reconsidered.[12] For Latin America, at least, guerrilla warfare did indeed gain some legitimacy because, it was explained, of the sociopolitical situation on that continent. Such a defense of guerrilla warfare occurred, however, primarily in arguments opposed to the idea of urban guerrilla warfare, which was deemed by Soviet theoreticians as virtually synonymous with "leftist terror." When juxtaposed with urban guerrilla warfare, so-called real guerrilla war was supported, but without seeming to change the overall preference for conventional warfare.[13]

If conventional warfare was preferred over guerrilla warfare, sabotage was clearly preferred over terrorism. A study by Defense Ministry and Africa Institute specialists praised what it presented as the choice made by movements in southern Africa for "underground sabotage activity" instead of terrorism. The logic of this choice, according to the authors, was that by hitting such infrastructure targets as industry and transportation, an outflow of capital from the area would sorely hurt the local regime.[14] Sabotage of government institutions and other centers of power "could inspire the masses" as well as exert pressure on the white public. This tactic was preferable to the use of terror because a "lack of human victims would avoid embittering the white population" and would allow for future cooperation. Yet, the study concluded, sabotage, much less terrorism, had "turned out to be ineffective, even for attracting the attention of the world public." Such actions were "used by the colonizers for propaganda sensations," and, in any case, international political and diplomatic pressures, in conjunction with internal pressures (political or military) produced greater results.[15]

This view was apparently standard Soviet thinking on the subject, for theoretical as well as pragmatic reasons. The Soviets perceived political change as the result of socioeconomic processes, with revolution occurring as an action of the people at the proper historical moment. Thus, any act of violence had to be systematic, directed toward precisely defined targets at a precisely defined time and possibly serving as a trigger for, or accompanying, the general armed uprising.[16] Acts of terrorism – by definition, indiscriminate blows against persons as well as property – were too diffuse to be effective in achieving overall sociopolitical change. Although theoretically they might serve to rouse the masses, attract international attention, and demoralize the ruling power or regime, Soviet theoreticians rejected these hypotheses. This position was found in specialized texts in Russian as well as in more general works, suggesting that it was not merely propaganda for foreign consumption.

Opposition to Terrorism

In the military, for example, Colonel Evgenii Dolgopolov explained that the choice of methods actually depended upon a number of factors, the major criterion being the extent and nature of social changes achieved—that is, their contribution to the "economic liberation and social progress" of the nation. Much also depended upon the "correlation of forces" in a particular country, the world arena, class and "other contradictions," colonial resistance and internal reaction, and the degree of violence used. The key for Dolgopolov was the massive character of the struggle; "national liberation uprisings and wars are massive, deeply popular movements having nothing in common with adventurist, conspiratorial acts, putschism, or terrorism," he argued. Rejecting the use of terrorism, he maintained that only mass action—a liberation army and guerrilla detachments operating with the essential element of broad popular support—could and did defeat the imperialists.[17]

Sobolev was more negative and explicit in his rejection of terrorism. Where earlier studies had considered terrorism counterproductive because the killing of civilians merely aroused hostility, Sobolev claimed that it was actually provocative as well as beneficial to the ruling class, which thus obtained a legitimacy for its use of repression.[18] On these grounds he opposed, for example, the "terrorist war against the staff of repressive apparatus" by the Tupermaros (Uruquayan urban guerrillas). In his book on left-wing terrorism, Viktor Vitiuk added that the alienation of the people from the would-be revolutionaries, as a result of tactics designed to create a psychological atmosphere of panic and fear, reduced the terrorists to small, isolated groups standing in opposition to the people, who were viewed merely as objects of manipulation.[19]

The *World Marxist Review* account of a 1979 conference on revolution and peace carried similar condemnations of terrorism. One participant condemned the use of terrorism by some in Western societies as the pursuit of "chimeras which have nothing in common with the complicated realities of the civil society and the revolutionary process."[20] An Irish participant, when asked about terrorism in Northern Ireland, was quoted as attributing the use of terrorism to the "disappointment of petty bourgeois groups in the possibility of attaining legitimate goals by means of the constitutional methods of bourgeois democracy, rejection of the forms and methods of the working-class struggle and refusal to carry on painstaking work among the masses." Explaining that this phenomenon had support among part of the population of Northern Ireland, as well as the Provisional Irish Republican Army (IRA), he added that the acts of terrorism "promote the growth of sectarian attitudes and prevent the establishment of an anti-imperialist alliance"; that is, these acts alienate people and set them against the cause. Moreover, "these acts enable the British government to intensify its repression on the plea that it is protecting the population." Arguing that terrorism was the symptom rather than the main problem (which was the need for fundamental change), he concluded the discussion: "Terrorism is the very opposite not only of democratic, but also of revolutionary, methods and goals of struggle."[21] This was just the point that Vitiuk dedicated most of his book to proving a few years later.

A number of these themes against terrorism were to be found in a 1983 article by Vladimir Fedorov, which also called terrorism counterproductive and identified the use of it with "left-wing extremists," citing the Red Brigade and Turkish terrorists.[22] Like Sobolev, Fedorov believed that acts of terrorism provide pretexts for the "repressive authorities [to] justify consolidation of the old and creation of new repressive bodies, the tightening of control over the population, restriction of the rights of the working people and broader, military interference of imperialists." Indeed, terrorism was so useful to the enemy that the latter even sought to gain control over "left-wing extremists (particularly terrorists)," so as to guide their actions in this provocative direction. An article in the military journal *Kommunist Vooruzhennykh Sil* claimed that the Red Brigade had been taken over by the United States and trained by the pro-Israeli South Lebanese Army.[23]

This last point was similar to claims made by Soviet observers that various acts of Palestinian terrorism were so counterproductive that they surely must have been the work not of Palestinians but of the Israeli secret service.[24] Indeed, there were a number of Soviet condemnations that Palestinian terrorism assisted the enemy and harmed the interests of the national liberation movement.[25] One of the rare references by a Soviet leader in the Brezhnev era to any specific form of armed struggle was just such a condemnation of a Palestinian terrorist act in 1972 by Gromyko speaking at the United Nations (UN).[26] Similarly, *Izvestiia* editor Lev Tolkunov, just before a visit of Yasir Arafat to Moscow in 1974, rejected the use of terrorism, recommending instead "proper forms" of struggle, such as sabotage against military targets.[27] It was in the guise of just such "sabotage against military targets" that the Soviet media presented those Palestinian acts of terror that it did not condemn outright.[28]

The Palestinian case occasioned more references to the issue of terrorism than would normally be found in Soviet sources. These references, unlike the comments contained in the more general discussions of armed struggle, did make some distinction between domestically employed terrorism and international terrorism. Neither was expressly condoned, but it was a great deal more difficult to portray international terrorism as sabotage or legitimate acts against military targets. Moreover, the Soviets may have felt no less vulnerable to hijackings, kidnappings, embassy occupation, and such than any other state—particularly after Lithuanian nationalists hijacked a Soviet airliner in 1970. At this time, the Soviets became more willing to support a strong UN General Assembly resolution against hijacking (in the face of opposition from some Third World states).[29] One can find nothing but Soviet condemnation for acts of international terrorism (on occasion before the resolution but in particular after its passage) no matter who was the perpetrator. On this matter, the Soviets' public position was clearly negative, despite their actual clandestine policies.

Public statements against any form of terrorism, more

clearly of a propagandistic nature, poured forth in a torrent in 1981, in response to U.S. accusations of Soviet support (and control) of international terrorism. There were innumerable direct assertions of Soviet opposition to terrorism, in principle and universally, by Soviet commentators and official sources, including an official TASS statement. Even such a leader as then Defense Minister Dmitrii Ustinov declared that

> terrorism is an instrument of extremism and neo-fascism, one of the most terrible manifestations of the moral and political crisis of capitalist society. . . .Terrorism is absolutely alien to socialism's very nature . . . the USSR has always been and remains an opponent in principle to the theory and practice of terrorism, including terrorism in international relations.[30]

Aside from propagandistic, defensive denials of this type, Soviet responses fell into two categories, neither of which defended the use of terrorism by anybody (despite the fact that in reporting specific terrorist acts of a national liberation movement in the past, they had occasionally expressed "understanding" for the use of such methods).[31] The responses in 1981 were either a defense of the national liberation movements' legitimate use of armed struggle, distinguishing such struggle from terrorism, or they were counteraccusations (not entirely new) that it was the imperialist states that were actually engaged in terrorism against innocent people.

Responding to earlier U.S. accusations, Colonel Dolgopolov had argued that national liberation movements rejected terrorism in favor of mass action for the simple reason that only the latter was effective against a colonial war machine.[32] However untrue this statement was regarding many movements, it was a rare attempt to provide what appeared to be a logical answer to Western accusations – an answer that reflected Moscow's own objections to the use of terrorism more than actual fact. It may have been Soviet sensitivity to the use of terrorism by some movements that prevented Soviet responses from following the Dolgopolov example or taking the trouble to explain the different forms of armed struggle and instead claim that national liberation movements did not use that particular form. Most Soviet responses simply claimed that Western accusations, which identified the national liberation struggle with the use of terrorism, including international terrorism, were merely designed to discredit the national liberation struggle and, indirectly, Soviet support for this struggle.

It was in this torrent of protestations of innocence that one could find Soviet condemnations of terrorism of the most general kind. These became somewhat more specific, elucidating the horrors and dangers of terrorism, when the second type of defense was employed – going on the offensive. This strategy consisted of arguing that it was in fact the imperialists who used "state terrorism . . . as part and parcel of [their] strategy of enslaving . . . the developing nations," including acts of terrorism against leaders of the national liberation movements.[33] This line was not fully expressed at the highest levels, but Gromyko did employ it indirectly when, at the UN, he countered U.S. charges of terrorism with accusations of U.S. support for "aggressor" policies and interference in the affairs of other peoples.[34] Speaking to the twenty-sixth CPSU Congress in 1981, Brezhnev chose not this response, but rather one that accused the West of maligning the national liberation movements; this accusation was included in his comments on the aggressive and interfering nature of U.S. policies.[35] Similarly, Brezhnev's message to the 1981 meeting of the Council of the Afro-Asian Solidarity Organization in Aden, South Yemen, combined both, a bit more explicitly; he accused the West of "widely using terror and violence against the fighting peoples" and stated that "the imperialists slander the national liberation movement by putting on it the label of 'international terrorism.'"[36]

In all of these charges, one thing was clear: The Soviet Union did not want to be accused of supporting terrorism or to admit that terrorism was used by groups that it was openly (as well as clandestinely) supporting. Whatever their attitude toward armed struggle, the Soviets obviously perceived that terrorism, particularly international terrorism, had nothing but negative connotations in the minds of most people in the world. It was probably this perception, rather than the military or ideological arguments invoked by some, that led to the view that the use of terrorism by revolutionary or national liberation groups was, on the whole, counterproductive. Just how much this view dictated actual Soviet behavior toward groups that use terrorism and just what role the Soviet Union actually played in the world arena of terrorism were other questions altogether.

2

Policy in the Brezhnev Era

A number of Western studies have provided ample evidence, as well as hearsay, to establish a link between the Soviet Union and international terrorism. Most focus on proving Soviet support to various groups or individuals involved in terrorism through the provision of Soviet arms, training, or propaganda. After demonstrating such links, which are particularly clear in the case of the Palestine Liberation Organization (PLO), some of these studies conclude that there is Soviet support for terrorism itself. From here, they often extrapolate to the idea of Soviet domination, control, and direction of terrorism.[1] Although some of the evidence presented in these studies is dubious and most agree that there is no firm evidence to link Soviet support or involvement with groups in Western Europe using exclusively terrorism, a few conclusions do appear to be valid.

First, the Soviet Union clearly — and in some cases rather openly — has provided arms to groups that practice terrorism. The presence of Soviet-bloc arms in the arsenals of various groups could be explained by the vast black market in arms, the independent transfer of arms by third parties, or even autonomous deals with some Communist countries — the last two actions not necessarily at the behest of Moscow or with Soviet agreement. Such explanations might account for the supply of Soviet-bloc arms via the Libyans and the PLO to the Soviet-opposed Moro National Liberation Front in the Philippines, the reported Polish shipment of arms to the contras in Nicaragua, or the Bulgarian arms-smuggling route to right-wing terrorist groups (and others) in Turkey.[2]

Nonetheless, Soviet arms were definitely supplied, even directly, to a number of groups that use terrorist tactics. Such supplies were barely hidden at the time, and most were openly admitted after independence, at least in the case of anticolonial national liberation movements in Africa. Treated by Moscow as anticolonial movements and acknowledged as receiving "all types" of Soviet aid, the PLO and the African National Congress (ANC) may also be included in this category. On occasion, a movement such as the separatist Kurds in Iraq received limited Soviet arms supplies, while others received what were most likely earmarked supplies (for example, the Tamils in Sri Lanka received supplies via the Indians, the Dhofaris in Oman via the South Yemenis, and the Polisario separatists in the Western Sahara via the Algerians). There were reports, difficult to confirm and from not particularly reliable sources about the supply of East European arms to the Italian Red Brigade and the Basque ETA (Euskadi Ta Askatasuna, or Basque Fatherland and Liberty Movement), either directly or earmarked through third parties.[3] Soviet-bloc arms were used by the Red Brigade in abducting Aldo Moro in 1978 and in attacking the Christian Democrats' Rome headquarters in 1979. Supplies of Czech-made arms reportedly reached them through Austria and Hungary, as well as from third parties, such as the PLO (primarily George Habash's Popular Front for the Liberation of Palestine or PFLP). The ETA was apparently in contact with Cuba, presumably receiving Soviet arms from that source.[4]

There were many reports that Soviet arms were supplied, usually indirectly, to the IRA.[5] Libya was the main conduit for these arms, although the PLO played a large role in the transfer of Soviet-bloc arms to the IRA. Soviet arms were also found in the arsenals of, were used by, or were intercepted en route to West German and Puerto Rican terrorist groups, Armenian terrorists from the Armenian Secret Army for the Liberation of Armenia (ASALA), the Japanese Red Army, the Colombian M-19, and the Sandinistas before their victory.[6] In many of these cases, the conduits were Libyan or Palestinian, as well as Cuban, North Korean, Algerian, or Vietnamese; whether they were acting at the behest of the Soviet Union remains unclear. The frequent use of Bulgaria for transfer of arms points to more direct Soviet involvement.

Second, the Soviet Union provided training for groups and individuals that subsequently used terrorist tactics. This training took place in the Soviet Union and Soviet-bloc countries (primarily Czechoslovakia, North Korea, and Cuba) and at various times in such third countries as Algeria, Egypt, Ethiopia, Syria, South Yemen, Angola (after independence), and North Vietnam. Soviet instructors from the KGB and apparently from the Soviet army's intelligence branch, GRU, provided the training much in the same manner that arms were supplied, with more consistent and open support going to the anticolonial movements in Africa, the PLO, and the ANC. Although more likely to receive training sporadically in third countries, separatists and revolutionaries may also have been trained in the Soviet Union and Eastern Europe. Kurds, Dhofaris, Colombians, Mexicans, Afghans (before 1978), and the infamous Venezuelan "Carlos" were among the many groups reportedly trained in the Soviet Union itself, while two of the later founders of the Red Brigade were trained in Czechoslovakia.[7]

Yet most revolutionary groups appear to have benefitted from Soviet training only secondhand through such Soviet clients as Libya, Cuba, or the PLO. Indeed, PLO cooperation with the West German Baader-Meinhof, the Italian Red Brigade, or the Japanese Red Army may have no more been at the behest of Moscow than was PLO aid to the pro-Chinese Burmese rebel groups or to the Eritreans or the Moros at times when the Soviets were actually opposed to these separatist groups. By the same token, training provided by Cuba and North Korea may not necessarily have been in every case a proxy action or a contrived cover for Soviet aid. Continued Cuban assistance to the Eritreans, for example, was opposed by Moscow and clearly contradicted the active post-1974 Soviet involvement in the Ethiopian military suppression of the Eritrean rebellion, attesting to the independent nature of some Cuban policies. Therefore, it cannot be ruled out that Cuban aid to radical groups in Central and Latin America, as well as to the ETA, has been conducted at least in part at Havana's own initiative.

Third, there have been no known cases that the Soviets refused to support, or suspended support for, a group because of its choice of methods—that is, its use of terror. A thorough study of Soviet support for national liberation movements revealed relatively clear criteria for Soviet policies, but the method employed by the movements was not one of them.[8] There was no change in the methods used by the Eritreans or the Kurds or the Tamils, for example, before the Soviet decisions to halt support; conversely, the adoption of more radical methods by the PLO or the ANC at various times prompted no alteration of Soviet support.

Rather, the Soviets often changed their characterization of the methods used when they decided to aid or cease aiding a movement; such was the case with the Eritreans, the Kurds of Iraq, the Tamils, and the PLO (and components of the PLO). The very same methods characterized as "resistance" or "guerrilla warfare" during periods of support were classified as "terrorism" during periods of nonsupport. By contrast, radical revolutionary movements—for example, the Red Brigade, Baader-Meinhof, and other groups that employed terrorist methods exclusively—were *not* treated ambiguously by Soviet media. Their methods were consistently characterized negatively as "terrorist." Although Moscow did not want to appear to be supporting these groups, their exclusive reliance on terrorism might have weighed against significant, direct Soviet support. The local, regional, and global factors that determined Soviet policies toward separatist movements probably played a greater role.

An exception to the above appears to be the IRA. Soviet media treatment of this movement and characterization of its terrorist activities were indeed ambiguous.[9] Condemnation of IRA terrorism could be found relatively frequently, and the term "terrorism" was employed. The Communist Party of Ireland was cited as "deploring the terrorist tactics of the Provisional IRA."[10] Yet some of these accounts softened this criticism by blaming the British for introducing terrorism into Northern Ireland, while others presented the struggle in Northern Ireland sympathetically, in anti-British terms, with no mention of IRA terrorism.[11] Still other accounts presented the IRA in a most favorable light, defending it against charges of terrorism.[12] In addition, Soviet studies on terrorism, such as Vitiuk's comprehensive volume *Leftist Terrorism*, ignored the IRA altogether as they chastised, in great detail, the Red Brigade, the West German Red Army Faction (RAF) and Baader-Meinhof, the ETA, the Japanese Red Army, Turkish terrorists, and a wealth of other revolutionary groups.

The fact that the Soviets armed and trained groups using terrorism and based their support on other factors did not mean that the Soviets had no preferences about methods; nor did it mean that there was no relation whatsoever between the expressed preferences of theoreticians and officials, on the one hand, and behavior in the field, on the other hand. There was evidence of disagreement between some movements and Moscow on the issue of armed struggle as such. In such cases, the Soviets apparently did not withhold political support and may even have knowingly supplied arms through a third party. Nonetheless, they counseled the Bengalis in East Pakistan, for example, and the Tamils (during a period of Indian, and therefore Soviet, support for the Tamils, including the more radical Tigers) to refrain from using force in any form in favor of political means. At certain times, during periods of Soviet political support similar advice was apparently also given to the separatist Eritreans, Kurds, and Baluchis of Iran and Pakistan, but the Kurds and the Eritreans, as well as the Pathans in Pakistan and the Dhofaris in Oman, also received some support for armed action. Indeed, in the case of the Kurds in Iraq and the Dhofaris, there was open Soviet support for armed struggle, accompanied by materiel assistance.

Soviet willingness to support, not merely tolerate, armed actions depended on calculations based on local, regional, and global interests, specifically Moscow's relationship with local and regional regimes, competition with the United States, and, to a much lesser degree, the Sino-Soviet dispute. Many of these interests presumably could be served, with little risk, by supporting armed struggle. The sporadic, often erratic nature of this support, however, suggests that the criteria for Soviet support depended on these variables rather than on Soviet preferences for particular means or estimates for success. Soviet support for the Dhofaris' armed struggle ceased, for example, when South Yemen terminated its involvement; Soviet support for the Tamils ended when the Indian government sent in a peacekeeping force that ultimately fought the Tamils; and Moscow even aided the armed suppression of both the Eritreans and the Iraqi Kurds when Soviet relations with the central governments involved were reversed.

The Soviets were much more willing to support armed struggle when it came to anticolonial movements. Even in these cases, however, their preferences were conveyed to the movements—for example, Soviet advice to the Vietcong to limit their military moves in favor of political efforts, or advice to the Popular Movement for the Liberation of Angola (MPLA) to agree to a coalition government rather than engage in a civil war upon independence. In the case of the MPLA, the movement was praised for refraining from the use of terrorism.[13] Despite preferences for political means, the road of prolonged armed struggle was admitted by the Soviets to be the only realistic option for the anti-Portuguese movements.[14] Some ambivalence was apparent in the Soviet attitude toward the armed struggle in Zimbabwe and Namibia, although on the whole armed struggle was supported even as political action was recommended as a parallel, occasionally preferable, means.

In Zimbabwe, the Soviet attitude toward the use of armed struggle by the Zimbabwe African People's Union (ZAPU), the movement supported by Moscow, was not entirely clear. Within Zimbabwe, one of the persistent complaints against ZAPU over the years, and one of the many factors leading to the creation in 1963 of a rival movement, the Zimbabwe African National Union (ZANU), was ZAPU's preference for political over military means.[15] ZAPU was generally much better armed (by the Soviets) than the Chinese-supported ZANU, but it was reluctant to engage in battle.[16] There was no indication, however, that this was necessarily the result of Soviet influence or preference. ZAPU was the first major movement in Zimbabwe to approach the Soviet Union before the ZANU break off, and there appeared to be agreement about the issue of political versus military means rather than one side's pressing the other or choosing the other for this reason. In an article criticizing ZANU, the Soviets accused the Chinese of inciting the Africans to armed struggle, and Moscow commended ZAPU's appreciation of the value of political means.[17] The armed actions undertaken by ZAPU together with the ANC of South Africa in 1967 were in fact uncharacteristic, both for ZAPU (and the ANC) and for the Soviet Union, particularly because they preceded rather than followed intensive political work. One observer has explained this anomaly by citing the Cuban concept of struggle, the dominant influence at the time.[18] In any case, the Soviets appeared to support, possibly even encourage, ZAPU leader Joshua Nkomo's pursuit of negotiations in 1974–1975.

On the other hand, in 1977, the Soviets were engaged in trying to convert the ZAPU military arm into a conventional force. This was in keeping with Soviet preferences for regular rather than guerrilla forces, though not necessarily an indication of actual intent to commit such forces in an all-out war. Indeed, as early as the 1967 joint ZAPU-ANC action, which was praised if not actually encouraged by Moscow, conventional rather than guerrilla techniques were used.[19] But there were also reports in 1977 that the Soviets were not only preparing for but actually encouraging such an offensive.[20] At this time, Moscow opposed the various negotiating efforts under way, and there were rumors that it might switch its support to Robert Mugabe's ZANU because this movement *was* willing to fight. *Pravda* even quoted Mugabe on the futility of political means (strikes, passive resistance) and the efficacy *only* of armed struggle.[21]

Although there is little evidence that the Soviets did in fact contemplate a shift to Mugabe, reportedly some Soviet officials (possibly members of the military mission sent to Zambia to reorganize ZAPU's army in 1978) did recommend such a switch, while others (including, perhaps, the Soviet ambassador to Zambia and Africanist Vassily Solodovnikov) persisted in their preference for political means.[22] In any case, Soviet propaganda from 1977 on spoke of the intensified armed struggle and generally condemned the various attempts at negotiations, although it also emphasized the desirability of a dual approach — both military and political means.[23] In fact, the Soviets appeared to favor negotiations on the whole, but not within the framework of those actually taking place — that is, under Western auspices. Similar ambivalence characterized their response to the Lancaster House talks in 1979, when Soviet media praised Zimbabwean flexibility but condemned the forum.[24] Moreover, there was not in fact any deployment of ZAPU forces in 1977 or after, and there were even subsequent reports of ZAPU dissatisfaction about Soviet arms deliveries. It is by no means certain, however, that the inadequacy of Soviet aid, if it in fact existed, was a form of Soviet pressure or an expression of Soviet hesitancy regarding armed struggle. Nkomo himself was apparently still opposed to a large military move. The Soviet media, in any case, never expressed any dissatisfaction with ZAPU's methods, referring to terrorist actions only generally, if at all, as acts of sabotage.[25]

A somewhat similar picture of Soviet ambivalence emerged in regard to the South West Africa People's Organization (SWAPO) armed struggle in Namibia. Moscow's involvement with SWAPO increased in the second half of the 1970s, as it did with all the African movements (this may have been due to the newly gained independence of the Portuguese colonies, which now facilitated the Soviet aid effort). By the mid-1970s, the Soviet media quoted SWAPO leaders to the effect that armed struggle was the "only" effective means. Some Soviet accounts were derogatory about negotiations, warning against what they called political maneuvers even while asserting that SWAPO was ready for talks at any time.[26] In the early 1980s, support for armed struggle became still more enthusiastic. Not only was guerrilla warfare against "industrial-military targets" praised, but SWAPO was said to have grown over the years from small detachments of guerrillas to a "people's liberation army conducting a 'real people's war.'" Nonetheless, most of these accounts spoke of simultaneous political work, even negotiations, although not negotiations of the type initiated by the West.[27]

There were some reports of a Soviet effort to restrain SWAPO from armed struggle in the late 1970s, ostensibly because of ideological disagreement or possibly because of a desire to await an end to the struggle in Zimbabwe. These reports occurred about the same time as a factional struggle within SWAPO over the issue of negotiations versus intensified armed struggle and about a challenge to Sam Nujoma's leadership as well.[28] It is not entirely clear, however, that Moscow sided with the majority favoring negotiation because at the time the Soviets were opposing the SWAPO-accepted UN Security Council Resolution 435 that called for a negotiated settlement. Moscow's opposition to this resolution was presumably based on the role designated for the West in the recommended independence process for Namibia. Its opposition was gradually replaced by Soviet support and even demands for negotiations based on implementation of the resolution in the early 1980s.

Similar ambiguity existed in the Soviet relationship with the ANC. Given the positive public pronouncements as well as the fact that South African Communists had created and remained the leadership core of the ANC's military wing Umkonto we Sizwe, Soviet support for armed struggle by the ANC was undeniable. Yet it was the ANC that developed an instrumental (catalyst) approach to armed struggle, the purpose of which was to spur a mass political movement rather than serve as the main means of struggle. For this reason, political means were deemed, at least by the Soviets, as equally important and even a priority. Evidence of this preference could be found in the accusations of a group that split off from the ANC in the mid-1970s, claiming, among other things, that the Soviets were trying to direct the movement toward diplomatic activity rather than armed struggle.[29]

During the 1984–1985 debate within the ANC about intensifying the armed struggle, in particular the use of terrorism (that is, "soft targets"), the Soviets apparently argued for political action. Soviet journal articles in the spring of 1985, just before the ANC Congress, spoke of both political and military struggle, noting political and organizational work and mass political action as the "most important" tasks, higher in priority than armed struggle.[30] Reporting on the congress itself, the Soviets referred indirectly to the debate, claiming that unity was preserved because of a decision "to step up the struggle," including the "broadening of the political and military offensive." Ignoring Western reports of the victory of those who had sought stepped-up violence, even to include soft targets (terrorism), the Soviets blithely placed "armed actions against apartheid" *last* in the list of actions (strikes and

protest demonstrations) praised at the congress for inspiring the masses.[31] Although this distortion of the pro-
ceedings presumably indicated Soviet preferences, the account did mention that the ANC rejected negotiations
"under present conditions."

The position of the South African Communists, specifically Joe Slovo, commander of Umkonto we Sizwe and the
first white elected to the ANC executive (at the same 1985
congress that accepted the more radical means of struggle),
was somewhat more ambiguous. Slovo reportedly opposed
the use of terrorism and had argued for political action. Yet
in an interview with a non-Soviet magazine a year later, he
spoke of the essential role played by "revolutionary violence" and of the justifiable possibility of hitting civilians
who were in the vicinity of military targets or who were
defined as military personnel because they belonged to
the "white farmer class."[32] Thus Slovo himself expressed
contradictory views, for even as he justified such actions,
he reiterated the need for a combination of political and
armed means. The same ambivalence could also be found in
the party's discussions, as "revolutionary violence" was
added to the recommended repertoire, alongside the emphasis on political work and action.

Soviet opposition to the use of armed struggle, and
particularly terrorism, on the part of the PLO was less ambiguous. Indeed, it was a source of tension between the two
at various times, erupting into open polemics between Moscow and George Habash's PFLP in the mid-1970s. Even
when the rift between Habash and Moscow was patched up
after the Camp David accords of 1978 and the PFLP began
to receive training in Cuba as well as Soviet assistance,
Moscow reportedly continued to try to restrain the group's
propensity for terrorism. Blanket opposition to armed
struggle of any kind may have been refined somewhat in the
1970s, when a distinction between terrorism and other
forms of armed struggle may have been introduced. Moscow reportedly urged Arafat to restrict armed activities to

sabotage and this within the occupied territories only.[33] The Palestine National Front (PNF), which was created, according to the Soviets, by a number of Arab Communist parties in 1973, was authorized to organize armed resistance against military targets in the occupied territories. Yet one of the reasons rumored for PLO refusal to accept the PNF into the PLO executive was its rejection of armed struggle.

A second reason was the PNF's preference for political accommodation with Israel, which reflected the other aspect of Moscow's position on the means to be used by the PLO. The Soviets pressured the PLO to opt for a political solution – that is, negotiations – and, for this purpose, they periodically urged PLO acceptance of Security Council Resolution 242. Such urgings disappeared when Moscow feared a shift by Arafat to U.S. mediation in 1977, for example, but the preference for political means over armed struggle, and especially over terrorism, remained. As in the case of the ANC, there were some apparent contradictions in the Soviet position regarding Palestinian terrorism, even of an international type. In the fall of 1973, terrorists from the Syrian-run Palestinian group Sa'iqa boarded a train in Czechoslovakia and carried out an operation against Soviet Jewish emigrants en route to the Vienna transit camp. Given controls in Czechoslovakia and the relationship of that country to the Soviet Union, there can be little question that the Soviets colluded in and possibly even initiated the operation, which would serve their interests regarding Jewish emigration (and coincide with Syria's interest in diverting attention from its forthcoming attack on Israel). Similarly, a number of East European countries were the departure points for heavily armed Palestinians en route to operations in the West, indicating logistical assistance as well as arms supplies.[34]

Overall opposition to terrorism, however, even when armed struggle was condoned or supported, remained relatively consistent. Soviet preferences about the type of armed struggle to be used were to some degree reflected in the qualitative nature of the support rendered. It would be difficult to distinguish clearly between sabotage and terrorism by the type of supplies or training given, but somewhat clearer distinctions could be made between supplies and training for sabotage and terrorism versus conventional warfare or even between guerrilla warfare and conventional warfare. Limited information available on the training provided by Moscow — documents found by the Israeli army in Lebanon, for example, or testimony made by former trainees from Afghanistan and other countries — clearly indicate that the training (use of explosives and so forth) was not only for sabotage but also for conventional warfare. Palestinians were trained to use heavy artillery, tanks, and even planes. Much of the equipment supplied reflected this as well. In fact, the Soviet Union undertook the conversion of the PLO armed units into a conventional army early in the 1980s. It reportedly attempted to do the same with the Dhofari rebels and, as noted above, with ZAPU fighters in the 1970s; it urged the African Party for the Independence of Guinea and Cape Verde (PAIGC), and possibly the Angolan MPLA and Namibia's SWAPO, to do the same during their liberation struggles.

None of this means that the Soviets were either ignorant or naive about the uses to which their training and arms were to be applied. Indeed, as pointed out above, the Soviets' objections to armed struggle or even to the use of terrorism did not apparently affect the degree of support rendered, including logistics as well as arms and training. They did affect the type of training rendered and, to some degree, the type of arms. Only in the case of groups using terrorism *exclusively* — revolutionary groups in Western Europe, Japan, and possibly Turkey — could a connection be drawn between Soviet reluctance to provide support and the tactics employed by the group. Yet in these cases as well, the absence or possibly minimal nature of Soviet support may have been the result of an entirely different set of considerations. Moreover, even in some of these cases, the

Soviet KGB maintained some contacts, seeking on occasion to influence operations in directions that coincided with Soviet interests, even when there was little or no approval of the methods employed or of the organizations themselves.

3

The Gorbachev Era

Regional Conflict

A sign that the new regime might be considering a change in its approach toward terrorism could be seen in a subtle addition to the definition of terrorism in the 1986 edition of the *Soviet Military Dictionary (Voyenni entsiklopedicheskii slovar')*. This definition added "new forms" of terrorism that, although generally credited to the West, nonetheless included for the first time hijackings, hostage taking, and similar acts that could no longer be attributed solely to regimes or oppressors acting against oppressed populations.[1] This was at least partial admission that groups struggling for power also used terrorism. The new wording actually followed the formulation presented by Gorbachev in his speech to the twenty-seventh CPSU Congress in February 1986. Gorbachev not only specified these and other types of terrorism, but also changed the context in which terrorism was treated. Instead of its former treatment as a part of accusations against the West or as a defense of national liberation movements, terrorism was now to be viewed as the result or side effect of regional conflicts and ongoing crises. As Gorbachev put it:

Crises and conflicts are also fertile ground for international terrorism. Undeclared wars, the export of counterrevolution in all its forms, political assassinations, hostage taking, aircraft hi-jackings, explosions in streets, airports, or railway stations – this is the loathesome face of terrorism, which those inspiring it try to disguise with various kinds of cynical fabrications.[2]

The significance of this shift was not at first apparent, except that the idea of "the export of counterrevolution" by the West, formerly expounded as the pretext for Soviet intervention in the Third World, was now relegated to this list of terrorist acts resulting from conflict situations. Although this did not signal the end of all accusations that the United States stood behind terrorism (indeed, even here the cynical fabricators were presumably Western sources), it did remove terrorism from the customary East-West propaganda battle and placed it in the much more significant realm of issues requiring solution.

The key here was the link with regional conflicts or ongoing crises. Basic to Gorbachev's new thinking in foreign policy is the tenet that the world's nations are in an interdependent relationship that belies the continuation of behavior patterns based on opposing camps, zero-sumgame thinking, and the Karl von Clausewitz dictum that war is politics in a different form. Soviet new thinking instead poses a model of universal interests to be achieved through a balance of particular interests. Inherent in this view is the idea that conflicts cannot be isolated in an interdependent world, the reaffirmed danger of escalation now being coupled with an expanded view of peaceful coexistence that envisions permanent East-West cooperation. The ramifications of this new thinking go far beyond these formulations to affect military doctrine, the concept of nuclear deterrence, the role of the Soviet armed forces, and Soviet relations with capitalist states, with the Third World as a whole, and with Communist parties.

At the same time, there is presumably a practical basis

for these ideas, stemming from domestic *perestroika* (restructuring). The monumental restructuring of Soviet society undertaken by Gorbachev requires a more economically sound foreign aid and trade program, economic-technological assistance from the capitalist world, and, perhaps most important, a respite from international tensions not only to facilitate these economic exigencies but also to redirect Soviet energies and resources to domestic tasks. Thus, whether for theoretical, practical—or even purely economic—reasons, regional conflicts and crises are to be avoided or eliminated.

Political versus Armed Struggle

The concern with and opposition to regional conflicts have given new importance, as well as priority, to discussions and stated preferences in regard to the issue of armed struggle versus peaceful means. Given the new theory of interdependence, it is no longer just a question of the dangers of escalation if outside powers become involved in regional conflicts—indeed, part of the new thinking argues that such conflicts are locally rather than globally generated. Rather, as a political observer in *Izvestiia* put it, "no one — and that includes local forces—can be freed from responsibility for the situation in a given area."[3] In this context, the use of violence by movements as well as states is condemned. Deputy Foreign Minister Vladimir Petrovskii thus explained that although some observers claim each component of the international system is autonomous, in fact "a comprehensive system of international security embraces all states and *public movements*."[4] Repeatedly specifying movements and "public forces" in addition to states, Petrovskii argued that all were obligated to seek solutions "by political means only, without resort to arms." In the spirit of glasnost, he also stated that this was no longer a matter of "preference" for political means as an "alternative" to military means, but an imperative. (Petrovskii even conceived it to be a moral as well as practical imperative, invoking Mahatma Ghandi and Leo Tolstoi on the use of nonviolence.)

Third World specialist Alexii Kiva placed the same dictum in a warning against blindly repeating the early Bolsheviks' use of "revolutionary violence," citing Lenin to the effect that "in the majority of civilized countries, such a bloody confrontation could be avoided." On this basis, Kiva criticized those who claimed that the achievement of revolutionary goals by means of negotiation, agreement, or compromise—rather than direct armed clashes with the class enemy—were reformist.[5] Soviet historian Evgenii Plimak was less emphatic about the Third World, but in connection with his own field—workers' movements in developed capitalist countries—he expressed the same admonition to rely exclusively on peaceful means, even when bringing about socialist revolution.

This was also the thrust of the advice given at a *World Marxist Review*-Latin American conference by the Soviet representative, Pavel Boiko (a section head from the Soviet Academy of Sciences' Latin America Institute). Boiko explained that the two victorious revolutions in the Western Hemisphere—Cuba and Nicaragua—had employed armed struggle because the regimes involved had not used political means but repression and terror. In the present circumstances, however, the opportunity for political reform and the introduction of democracy should be used, not scorned. "It is in the interests of the working people to get rid of authoritarian regimes, and here struggle for civil liberties and democracy is the best weapon. Every step taken by the people towards democracy, even if it is bourgeois democracy, means a retreat of the social classes enjoying privileges under dictatorial regimes."[6]

Evgenii Primakov, promoted under Gorbachev to the prestigious position of director of the Institute of World Economy and International Relations and to candidate member of the Central Committee and later elected head of a chamber of the new Soviet parliament, is a key theoretician of the new thinking. As former head of the Oriental

Institute, where he was a Third World and Middle East expert, Primakov has accompanied Gorbachev on a number of trips and appears to have a say in the formulation of Soviet foreign policy toward the Third World, if not more generally. Indeed, the promotions he received indicate an acceptance of the theoretical premises he espoused over the years. In the May 1988 issue of *Mezhdunarodnaia zhizn'*, Primakov attempted to elucidate certain aspects of the new thinking, specifically the opposition to the use of force, in relation to the question of armed struggle and just wars for national or social liberation.[7] There is a hint in this article of the Brezhnev era's "divisibility of détente"—that is, accommodation at the superpower level but support for continued revolutionary activity by any means at the level of movements. At the same time, there is also the hint of the old pro-détente argument that the restraining features of détente would prevent Western interference, thereby eliminating any need for force by internal elements.

Primakov claimed that to prevent a contradiction between the new thinking and the legitimate right of national and social liberation movements to use any means, one must more precisely define the concepts of export of revolution and export of counterrevolution. If what he called the "adventuristic and ultra-revolutionary" ideas fostered by those advocating the export of revolution were completely abandoned, there would no longer be a pretext for Western intervention in the form of the export of counterrevolution ostensibly to fight external (Soviet) support for revolutionaries. Conflicts would therefore be reduced to their internal causes, which could and should be dealt with only by non-military means. "National reconciliation" (the term used mainly for ending rebellions against Soviet-supported regimes) could provide the peaceful solution once external elements were removed from the equation. Political means, Primakov claimed, should also be used "to eliminate the internal causes of regional conflicts where two or several nations are involved," although in the case of interstate conflict, only defensive wars could be qualified as just wars.

Allowing that no one could impose a particular form of struggle on national liberation conflicts, Primakov spoke of the need for "enhanced responsibility" for those involved in such struggles. Thus he concluded: "In general . . . military means should never be used to eliminate the causes of conflicts, whatever they may be."

This position was reiterated with increasing clarity and vehemence. It was also increasingly tied to criticism of past Soviet policies and theoretical convolutions. Viktor Kremeniuk of the Academy of Sciences' Institute for the Study of the USA and Canada, who was a pre-Gorbachev supporter of a more restrained Soviet foreign policy, told a Foreign Ministry–*Mezhdunarodnaia zhizn'* symposium that not a "single postwar conflict has been settled by military means even where no great powers were involved. Nor could it have."[8] Claiming that "we misled even ourselves," he criticized the Soviet Union's formula of "just and unjust wars." This formula, which had been invoked to justify wars of national liberation, was dismissed by Kremeniuk as having merely provided the basis upon which Moscow "found a loophole for a positive attitude to the use of military force and actually used it."

A slightly different but equally critical line of argument appeared to be the one used by Richard Ovinnikov, director of the State Institute for International Relations and member of the Collegium of the Foreign Ministry. He made the notable admission that it had been a "miscalculation" to believe that détente could be maintained, even extended, despite Moscow's "growing involvement in regional conflicts, albeit on the side of a just cause."[9] This was not the opinion of some contributors in a joint symposium conducted by the journal *Mezhdunarodnaia zhizn'* and the Academy of Social Sciences (a generally conservative institute belonging to the CPSU Central Committee's Ideological Department) on the eve of the June 1988 CPSU Conference. Nonetheless, one analyst from the party's academy, Professor Aleksandr Migolatev, offered Afghanistan as proof that "internal conflicts due to interclass, national, ethnic or religious causes are apt to greatly aggravate the situation, not only in a subregion or region, but throughout the world. A local conflict tends to internationalize armed struggle, with all ensuing consequences." Championing "national reconciliation" as a means of solving "class, political and ideological problems in terms of giving priority to the interests of peaceful development," Migolatev concluded that any struggle against conservative, reactionary forces "should be carried on along new lines and take new, *nonmilitary and more civilized forms*."[10]

Andrei Kozyrev, a Foreign Ministry official (deputy head of the Department for International Organizations) and believed to be close to Eduard Shevardnadze, echoed Ovinnikov when he criticized "our direct or indirect entanglement in regional conflicts [that] brings about enormous losses, exacerbating overall international tensions, justifying the arms race and hampering mutually beneficial economic ties with the West." He described as "outdated" the view that relations between the West and the Third World were looked at "through the prism of 'suppressing national liberation aspirations.'" According to Kozyrev,

> "Anti-imperialism" is a poor counsellor in matters related to improving the situation in the world as a whole and in some of its parts. De-ideologizing [sic] international relations calls for the primacy of law, which is the best constraint of aggressive designs. . . . As to attempts to export counter-revolution to the developing world sphere, such violence should be barred by an international peace-keeping mechanism and, what is no less important, by the in-depth analysis in each case of both the essence of internal processes and the nature of external threat.

In what was basically an explanation of the possibilities for East-West cooperation and an end to rivalry, Kozyrev opposed not only the export of revolution on the part of Moscow, but demanded that local revolutions defend themselves, by themselves, "and above all by non-military means."[11]

Writing for a foreign audience in the *World Marxist Review*, while still party secretary for foreign affairs and head of the International Department of the Central Committee, Anatolii Dobrynin spoke in terms somewhat similar to those of Kozyrev. Denying that the effort to find political solutions to regional conflicts meant Soviet abandonment of "solidarity with the people's liberation struggle," Dobrynin subtly changed an old formula by saying that Moscow countered the export of counterrevolution "with the principle of law." The implication was that law, rather than arms, was the answer.[12]

Summing up the foreign policy lines adopted by the party at the June 1988 conference and amplifying themes introduced by Gorbachev, Shevardnadze specified the "exclusive supremacy of political means over all other vehicles for handling international affairs."[13] He gave this a more pragmatic twist when he criticized the lack of coordination between the military and political components of Soviet diplomacy in the past, when an overemphasis was given to the military. Concluding that wars had rarely if ever achieved "any solid political or other results," he said that war and armed conflicts in the nuclear age lose their rational function. With regard to internal and national liberation struggles, the Soviet foreign minister offered the examples of "national reconciliation" in Afghanistan and the political solutions being applied to such problem areas as Namibia. He argued that Moscow did not export revolution, adding that the Soviet Union had to observe the norms of morality if it wanted to be accepted as part of the civilized world community.[14]

The authoritative position most often referred to was the Delhi Declaration on Principles for a Nuclear-Weapon Free and Non-Violent World, which was promulgated at the close of Gorbachev's visit to India in November 1986. This document called for the resolution of conflict situations "through peaceful, political means, not through military means."[15] This was, of course, a very general formulation, which could and was easily applied specifically to Western interventions or Western-supported rebellions. Nonetheless, Gorbachev frequently reiterated this formula, and, on some occasions, he applied it directly to specific struggles such as that of the blacks in South Africa.[16] Like Brezhnev before him, Gorbachev rarely spoke of armed struggle as such; unlike Brezhnev, however, Gorbachev did not use the "divisibility of détente" idea. In Gorbachev's formula, no conflict, whatever its source or purpose, was excluded from the decree for exclusive – not merely preferential – use of peaceful rather than military means.

Views of the Military

The principle of preferring political rather than armed means was supported by some in the military as well, although far less consistently or frequently. There were general statements rejecting war as a means of settling disputes of any type. Explanations of the new Soviet military doctrine's emphasis on defense usually included such proclamations, with particular reference to interstate conflicts. Journals intended for a foreign audience, such as *New Times* and the *World Marxist Review*, carried, for example, an interview with First Deputy Chief of the Soviet Armed Forces Colonel General Vladimir Lobov and an article by Chief of the General Staff Marshal S. F. Akhromeyev, both declaring socialism's "unconditional" rejection of war as a means of resolving interstate conflicts.[17] Colonel General Dmitrii Volkogonov, then deputy chief of the Main Political Directorate of the Army and Navy (later named head of the Defense Ministry's History Department and charged with writing a study of Stalin), eventually described this as an antiwar doctrine.[18]

It was more significant, however, to find even such general statements in military media. Colonel B. Lytov, for example (identified only as a candidate of historical sciences), wrote in *Aviatsiya i kosmonavtika* that the military doctrine adopted by the Warsaw Pact in May 1987 included a rejection of the use of military force; Army General A. I. Gribkov, Warsaw Pact chief of staff, told a *Krasnaia zvezda* interviewer that the only way to avert destruction of the human race in the nuclear age was to "rule out force and the threat of its use from interstate relations and resolve all disputes by political means."[19] Western expert Raymond Garthoff has documented this aspect of the new Soviet military doctrine as it has appeared in the important, restricted Soviet military journal *Voennaia mysl* as well as in other Soviet military sources.[20]

The most authoritative military expression of this view would be, in addition to the May 1987 Warsaw Pact resolution, an article by Soviet Defense Minister Army General D. T. Yazov, in which he stated that the "cardinal task" of Soviet military doctrine was "not permitting war, nuclear or conventional."[21] It was not clear that this was meant to apply to armed struggle by revolutionary or national liberation movements as well as to interstate conflict and Soviet doctrine. In his book *On Guard over Socialism and Peace*, Yazov spoke of the dangers of "armed conflicts (local wars)" that could "grow into a world war with all its consequences. Therefore, modern warfare threatens the destruction of mankind. This is why it cannot be an extension of prudent and responsible policy."[22] Yet he attributed these armed conflicts to imperialism, providing no indication as to whether the same principle applied to revolutionary and national liberation armed struggles.

There was, however, one clearer indication that this did apply to such struggles. It came from Major General Evgenii Dolgopolov, who just a year earlier had taken the opposite position. Writing in *Krasnaia zvezda* in June 1988 about the new possibilities for resolving regional conflicts through U.S.-Soviet cooperation, he said: "The nuclear era requires that revolutionary forces in every country show a maximum of balanced judgment in making decisions regarding an armed struggle, that they reject on principle

different expressions of leftist extremism."[23] It is difficult to
determine just how important Dolgopolov is among the military, but he has for years been a frequent and even major
military commentator on Soviet policy in the Third World
and the national liberation struggle.

It appears, however, that the new thinking was not accepted by all the military, given the number (albeit dimin-
ishing) of articles pointing to the continued aggressiveness
of the West.[24] One military commentator even quoted Lenin
to the effect that "warfare is rooted in the very essence of
capitalism."[25] Another, attempting to demonstrate the foi-
bles involved in subordinating military to political solutions, invoked Stalin's failure to prepare for the German
attack of 1941.[26] Some of these arguments pointed to the
continued aggressiveness of the West in the Third World,
which necessitated that the Soviet armed forces maintain
an "external function" to counter the export of counterrevolution.[27] These commentators criticized implicitly, if not explicitly, the idea of political rather than peaceful solutions,
given, they claimed, the persistence of imperialist military
intervention. There were few commentators, however, who
directly and positively addressed the issue of armed struggle in the Third World or elsewhere.

One exception was Major Nikolai Efimov, described by
Kommunist vooruzhennykh sil only as a candidate in phi-
losophy. Expressing Communist preferences for peaceful
means, he defended the rights of oppressed peoples or classes to conduct armed struggle rather than negating violence
unconditionally. He argued that imperialist efforts to prevent social change often left the workers no choice but the
use of arms. Clearly defending the idea of armed struggle,
he nonetheless concluded that the best strategy would be
an "expert combination of peaceful and non-peaceful
means."[28] Writing in 1986 and early 1987, Volkogonov took
a stronger line in this same direction. At that time, he cited
Lenin to the effect that "there are 'wars and wars,'" explaining that "Marxists do not condemn war in general. That
would amount to pacifism. Our support will always be with

those nations who conduct a just struggle for social and national liberation, against imperialist domination and aggressions."[29] By June of 1987, however, Volkogonov was advocating what he called the "New Thinking's Anti-War Doctrine."

Dolgopolov, too, initially championed the armed struggle position, like Volkogonov only gradually accepting the new thinking. Writing in July 1987, Dolgopolov strongly and explicitly defended armed struggle by national and social movements against imperialism, exploitation, or the export of counterrevolution.[30] Even more clearly than Volkogonov, he justified such warfare despite the dangers of escalation. As late as April 1988, Dolgopolov was still writing about the continued aggressiveness of imperialism, which prevented peaceful solutions—that is, "national reconciliation"—to local conflicts.[31] Yet, by June 1988, he was finally willing, in *Krasnaia zvezda*, to counsel second thoughts regarding armed struggle and demand the rejection of extremism on the part of liberation movements.

Soviet Military Review appears to have been the spokesman for support of armed struggle and, perhaps, a last bastion of opposition to the new thinking. Inasmuch as it is published in English and, therefore, intended for overseas consumption, it may be argued that its task is to ensure overseas readers that Moscow has not abandoned either its support for local struggles or its place in the world. Yet, whatever propaganda function this journal may serve, the fact that it sought to convey a particular message to movements or groups overseas cannot be ignored. This message has included not only Efimov and Dolgopolov's impassioned support for armed struggle. In April 1988, an anniversary tribute to Marx spoke of Marx's rejection of "a pacifist denial of war" and noted his support for "the right of the working class and oppressed peoples to armed fighting against acts of violence on the part of the oppressor both at home and abroad, and the right to revolutionary wars." Asserting the relevance of Marx's views today, the article maintained the validity of "the Marxist-Leninist argument that nations' armed fighting against imperialist aggression is their legitimate right. . . . "[32] The following month, the same journal published an article praising the use and tactics of partisan warfare in World War II, and it carried an answer to a reader's letter denying any contradiction between the Soviet Union's search for political solutions to conflict and its continued nonpolitical (that is, military) assistance "to the oppressed and those who need protection [sic] from imperialist expansion."[33]

4

A New Approach to Terrorism

Condemnation of Terrorism

Although the official, increasingly supported Soviet position ruled out armed struggle, even those who continued to support it (or tolerate it, albeit as an unpreferred alternative) opposed the use of terrorism. As in the pre-Gorbachev period, there were those, particularly in the military, who strove to distinguish between the various forms of armed struggle, supporting guerrillas, for example, while condemning terrorism. The defense of armed struggle by Major Efimov included the claim that "sometimes guerrilla [the Russian word is *partizan*] struggle is the only way for social and national liberation." Efimov went on to say, however, that "there is no connection between the real revolution and the armed actions of left-wing extremists. These kinds of activities characterize the political adventures of neo-Trotsky groups, left-wing and otherwise, which directly and indirectly aid big capital."[1] Dolgopolov attacked U.S. labeling of national liberation movements as "international terrorists," arguing that "true revolutionaries have always made a clear distinction between terror and popular armed struggle against imperialist aggressors or [sic] inner counter-revolution."[2] At an *Izvestiia*-sponsored roundtable entitled "Terrorism—An Instrument of Neoglobalism," legal specialist Lidiia Modzhoryan also defended the legal rights of "victims of aggression and members of anticolonial and antiracist movements to wage armed struggle," but she listed certain actions that were banned "for all time and for everyone." These actions included "violence against civilian populations, barbaric treatment of prisoners of war, torture, setting off of explosions, aircraft hi-jacking, and so on."[3] Such discussions are rare, however, primarily because the defense of armed struggle itself has become increasingly rare.

Far less explicit, and far less convincing, were the occasional assertions that the "legitimate struggle" conducted by national liberation movements could not be termed terrorism.[4] Thus the PLO was said to be waging a legitimate armed struggle that had no connection with terrorism—although the publicly added caveat on one occasion was that it would be preferable to conduct this struggle within the occupied territories and not against civilian targets outside the territories.[5] Similarly *Pravda*, condemning a wave of terrorist incidents in France in the fall of 1986, asserted that "lone fanatics cannot be placed on the same footing with the peoples who struggle for emancipation."[6] These claims fell into the category of accusations often heard in the West—that one person's terrorist is another person's freedom fighter. Actually, one Soviet commentator reversed this, aiming the accusation at the United States for presumably "describing the Contras and the Dushmans as 'freedom fighters' and the Governments of Nicaragua and Afghanistan as 'terrorists.'"[7]

Such comments about the U.S. attitude toward terrorism were part of the usual counteraccusations frequently employed by the Soviets, particularly after 1981. Like the defense of armed struggle, this type of argument diminished significantly by 1987 and almost disappeared entirely. As late as 1986, however, there were frequent sallies against the United States (and against Israel even into 1988) for conducting "state terrorism." According to one theme, the minute the international climate improved (presumably in U.S.-Soviet relations), the reactionary forces in Washington would trot out the old cold war accusations against Moscow, including charges that the Soviet Union was behind international terrorism.[8] Thus, both *Izvestiia* and *Pravda* righteously denied, for example, French allegations of Bulgarian involvement in terrorist attacks that had occurred in Paris.[9]

It was most common, however, to convert any report on terrorism to accusations that the right-wing, particularly the United States, was in fact the culprit, even if only indirectly. The argument was that the scourge of terrorism was to be treated at its roots, and its roots were imperialism, colonialism, racism, and, of more recent vintage, neoglobalism. Even Gorbachev made this connection during his trip to India in 1986.[10] The United States, it was said, practiced "state terrorism" as part of its neoglobal policies, and this in turn prepared the ground for individual terrorism, for "wherever some forms of terrorism are officially sanctioned and supported, it will also emerge in other forms."[11] Gorbachev's CPSU Congress definition of terrorism was thus explained in a fashion limited to the West; according to *Izvestiia*, "crises and conflicts [Gorbachev's words] are rich soil for international terrorism. Undeclared wars and the export of counterrevolution in all forms are very dangerous manifestations of the state terrorism practiced by the United States. Terrorism begets terrorism."[12]

This line was reiterated in response to a U.S. Senate bill permitting the prosecution of terrorists involved in attacks on U.S. citizens abroad. Counterattacking, the Soviets frequently pointed out that the United States had given refuge to two Soviet citizens, a father and son, who had hijacked a Soviet plane in 1970, killing a stewardess and injuring others. This was amplified by accusations that the United States was harboring "well paid terrorist gangs."[13] Examples of U.S.-sponsored "state terrorism" were an even more frequent part of Moscow's attacks, particularly with regard to U.S. campaigns against Libya and, occasionally,

Syria. U.S. accusations and moves against Libya were declared mere provocations, sometimes said to be instigated together with Egypt or with Israel, and designed variously to overthrow Mu'ammar Qadhafi, to force acceptance of a U.S.-Israeli *diktat* in the Middle East, to divide the Arab world, to create tension and deterioration of the situation in the Middle East, to teach the Arabs (of all persuasions) a lesson, to flex the U.S. muscle, to frighten the antiwar forces in the world, or all of the above.[14]

Although Britain was briefly included in these accusations when it moved against Syria for its role in attempting to blow up a plane at Heathrow Airport, Israel was the main target of Soviet statements against "state terrorism." Indeed, Soviet accusations against the United States virtually disappeared from Soviet media after 1986 (returning only briefly in August 1988 in response to the publication of the State Department's report, *Patterns of Global Terrorism*, 1987), which left Israel to take the brunt of subsequent Soviet attacks.[15] Except for the response to Abu Jihad's assassination in Tunis in 1988, however, the attacks were not particularly extensive. There were brief reports of Jewish Defense League (JDL) or "extremist Zionist" acts in the United States or Europe, as well as condemnations of Israeli army moves against Palestinian bases or infiltrators. Gorbachev did speak of "Tel Aviv's campaign of terror" against the Palestinians, and, in 1988, a Ukrainian book on terrorism was almost entirely dedicated to virulent attacks against alleged Zionist or Israeli acts of terror.[16] These and other accusations linked the Mossad to much of world terrorism, but even these attacks appeared to decline as Soviet-Israeli relations improved during 1987–1988.[17]

There was, by and large, little change in the overall condemnation of terrorism. Discussions of the issue continued to criticize left-wing as well as right-wing extremists, even as the old accusations against the West were maintained.[18] One notable contribution was that of Soviet terrorism specialist Andrei Grachev, who effectively listed all the counterproductive consequences of terrorism, once again condemning the "'brigades,' 'fronts,' 'proletarian cells,' and 'red army factions.'" He described these as "having broken with social movements, having come out as the sworn enemies of the working class, its trade unions and political parties, and set themselves in opposition to the state and society."[19] Grachev also condemned "state terrorism" conducted by the United States and Israel, but he did so in a context that barely distinguished between what he called "terrorists and counter-terrorists." Without saying it, perhaps without intending it, he generalized from incidents that were also perpetrated by national liberation movements, labeling them all "terrorism."

This was, in fact, one new feature of the Soviet attitude toward terrorism. The reporting and discussion of incidents showed signs that the usually clear distinctions were blurring between the methods used by "terrorists" and by those fighting imperialism; the term "terrorist" no longer exclusively described incidents perpetrated by groups opposed by Moscow. The bombing of the West Berlin discotheque, which was aimed at U.S. servicemen, was condemned, for example, as terrorism in April 1986, despite the fact that it was perpetrated by Palestinians. Once the United States accused Libya of complicity, however, the Soviets reverted to the old ploy of claiming that the attack had been a Central Intelligence Agency (CIA)-Mossad provocation.

Nevertheless, a few months later there was a particularly strong Soviet reaction to an incident in the Karachi airport in which Palestinian terrorists seized a U.S. commercial airliner, which resulted in the death of some 20 persons. A TASS statement declared that the Soviet Union "decisively condemns this terrorist act," adding that "there can be no justification for this act, and those who committed the crime, *no matter what motives guided them*."[20] Although the identity of the terrorists was not mentioned, the fact that they were from the Abu Nidal faction rather than from a group directly supported by Moscow may have affected the Soviet response. Yet a later Palestinian attack on a group of Israeli recruits and their families after a swearing-in ceremony in Jerusalem was described as a "terrorist" operation, despite the fact that the target was a military one.[21] Although not all Palestinian attacks were thus described, the use of the term "terrorist" for Palestinian operations was to repeat itself. The attack on a Greek cruise ship in July 1988, which resulted in the death of nine persons, was also condemned as terrorism without identifying the terrorists. More significant was the October 1988 bombing of a civilian Israeli bus in Jericho (in the occupied territories); it was also described as a "terrorist" act in a condemnation issued by Foreign Ministry spokesman Gennadii Gerasimov.[22]

Not only Palestinian incidents were condemned. In March 1988, the apparently more conservative *Soviet Military Review* spoke of "terrorist gangs" that intimidated the civilian population in Northern Ireland, making the situation there "still worse."[23] The unsigned report concluded that the "sad outcome" of such events was merely more civilian victims "followed by a fresh crackdown by the police and military — fresh aggravation of the situation." Such unambiguous condemnation, refraining from any "understanding" of what was a clearly counterproductive tactic, had not been characteristic of earlier Soviet reporting of events in Northern Ireland.

Similarly, *Izvestiia* described "terrorist" attacks in Khartoum in May 1988, as well as a number of what it called "terrorist" incidents in Lebanon, including the kidnapping of two Americans in January 1987.[24] Many of the Lebanese incidents were conducted by Islamic groups, the actions of which were usually condemned by Moscow, even when they occurred in Egypt or against Western targets.[25] Nonetheless, the pattern seemed to be one of Soviet opposition to kidnappings, no matter who the perpetrator. Indeed, an extraordinary expression of sympathy for U.S. hostage Terry Anderson, being held in Lebanon, was published in *Sovetskaia rossiya* in June 1988. The Soviet paper urged Anderson to be strong, and it promised punishment for the abductors.[26] Following a similar pattern, opposition to air-

line hijackings was consistent, as evidenced by the condemnation of "terrorists" who hijacked an Air Afrique plane in
July 1987 and, especially, the "criminal terrorist" hijacking
of a Kuwaiti airliner in April 1988.[27] The April hijacking
prompted a number of Soviet condemnations of terrorism
in general, including one by commentator Viktor Lebedev:

> No few acts of terrorism were staged in the Middle
> East in the course of recent years, whose aim was the
> fight against Israel and against the interests of imperi-
> alism in the region. Terrorism, a means which is unwor-
> thy of the aim, distorts these aims themselves . . . as a
> result of their [terrorists'] criminal actions, innocent
> people are killed, the number of victims grows, dramas
> take place, but as a result only the sides advocating
> violence stand to gain. The insane labyrinth of terror
> ends up in the impasses of immorality.[28]

International Cooperation

There were other signs that the new thinking contained a
new approach to terrorism. As early as the end of 1985, well
before the indications of a change regarding armed struggle
in general, the Soviet Union changed its position in the
United Nations. For the first time, on December 6, 1985,
the Soviet bloc voted with the United States in the General
Assembly (in a vote of 118 to 1) and later in the Security
Council for resolutions condemning as "criminal" all acts of
terrorism "from whatever source."[29] The General Assembly
resolution called for the strengthening of measures to "facilitate the prevention, prosecution and punishment of all acts
of hostage-taking and abduction as manifestations of international terrorism."[30] It had been preceded two months earlier by Soviet agreement to a Security Council statement
(not resolution) condemning the terrorist attack on the
Achille Lauro and terrorism "in all its forms, wherever and
by whomsoever committed."[31] Neither the resolution nor the

earlier statement included any reference to the "state terror-ism" always insisted upon by the Soviet bloc in the past.

Such a turnabout, after years of haggling and reticence in the UN committee on terrorism created in 1972, may have been prompted by the kidnapping of four Soviet diplo-mats in Beirut three months earlier (and the killing of one of them). It was also, however, a harbinger of the policy to be announced by Gorbachev at the February 1986 CPSU Con-gress, in which the new Soviet leader called for the "drawing up of effective measures for preventing international terror-ism, including security for the use of international land, air, and sea communications."[32] Indeed, according to some re-ports, Gorbachev had already raised the subject with Presi-dent Ronald Reagan at the Geneva summit in November 1985, promising more than mere declarations. The subse-quent UN resolution reportedly was agreed to in principle by the two leaders at that time.[33]

In 1987, Gorbachev again spoke about the subject, ex-panding slightly on the direction he intended the Soviet Union to take. Once again he condemned "crises and con-flicts [as] the seedbed for international terrorism" and linked the elimination of the phenomenon to the elimination of the reasons for the conflicts themselves:

> The Soviet Union rejects terrorism in principle and is prepared to cooperate energetically with other states in eradicating this evil. It is expedient to concentrate this work within the United Nations. It would be useful to establish under its aegis a tribunal for investigating acts of international terrorism. During a bilateral dia-logue with the Western countries (in the past year there was a major exchange of views on this score between us and the USA, Britain, France, Federal [Republic of] Germany, Italy, Canada and Sweden) we came out for the elaboration of effective measures to combat terror-ism. We are prepared to conclude special bilateral agreements. I hope that the common struggle against international terrorism will broaden in the years to come.[34]

In keeping with this position, Soviet commentators had already begun to call for concrete measures to combat terrorism, even as they continued their customary accusations against the West, the CIA, and the Israeli Mossad. In the *Izvestiia* roundtable entitled "Terrorism — An Instrument of Neoglobalism," for example, Soviet experts called for interstate cooperative measures to cover such things as extradition and acceptance by all states of the agreements already reached on combating international terrorism.[35] Extradition was one of the first issues raised in this new approach probably, although not always directly, because of the U.S. refusal to extradite the 1970 hijackers of a Soviet plane. The head of the law department of the Soviet Research Institute for Civil Aviation, for example, spoke of the need for mandatory extradition of hijackers, but he also referred to the UN General Assembly resolution adopted a few months earlier and called for more stringent security measures at airports and aboard aircraft. He cited the 1983 Turkish imprisonment of two hijackers of a Soviet plane as another positive example of how to deal with such crimes.[36] Israel's swift return of the Soviet hijackers of a plane to Tel Aviv in December 1988 was repeatedly cited by Soviet media as an example of the way in which such incidents should be treated. The full cooperation of the states involved, as well as the speedy extradition of the terrorists, was copiously praised.

The Soviets apparently took concrete steps to implement the proposed cooperation. On April 23, 1986, they denied West German reports that Moscow had supplied Bonn with a list of some 30 Palestinian terrorists following the *Achille Lauro* hijacking a year earlier. Yet another Western source claimed that Moscow had given French intelligence a list of names of terrorists.[37] Some cooperation apparently did begin to develop, particularly with regard to terrorism in West Germany. At a meeting of U.S. and East German Foreign Ministry officials in May 1986, the East Germans undertook a commitment to prevent embassies located in East Germany from being used as bases for terrorist operations (as the Libyan embassy had been used in preparations to attack the West Berlin discotheque during the previous month).[38] The East Germans, with Soviet involvement, appeared to be fulfilling this commitment when, according to Western sources, they responded to U.S. warnings about the presence in East Berlin of a suspected Libyan diplomat. The Soviets, according to one report, informed the Americans that the Libyan would be told to leave, and he apparently did leave. This action, in direct contrast with the Soviet–East German refusal to respond to similar warnings before the West Berlin discotheque bombing, was cited by U.S. diplomats in West Berlin as a sample of the more cooperative behavior of the Soviets and East Germans.[39]

In fact, East European cooperation on terrorism reportedly caused the U.S. government not to publish a study originally designed to expose East European assistance to Abu Nidal.[40] According to the same source, this cooperation went so far as to include an East European tour by State Department counterterrorism official Alvin Adams and an exchange of information on antiterrorist techniques. Soviet-British talks for cooperation between their two countries on such issues were also reportedly agreed upon at the end of 1986.[41]

In January 1989, following Israeli cooperation with Soviet authorities and the return of Soviet hijackers immediately after they had landed their plane in Tel Aviv, Deputy Director of the KGB Lt. Gen. Vitali Ponomariev expressed KGB willingness to work with other intelligence services on this matter. In an unprecedented statement from a representative of the one body that could "make or break" Gorbachev's peaceful overtures in this realm, Ponomariev said: "We realize we have to coordinate efforts to prevent terrorist acts, including hijackings of planes. . . . We are willing, if there is a need, to cooperate even with the CIA, the British Intelligence Service, the Israeli Mossad, and other services in the West."[42] A contributing factor to this new attitude may have been the fact that Israel had permitted a high

KGB officer to come to Tel Aviv to arrange the return of the hijackers and aircraft during the December incident.

In 1987, the Soviet Union undertook something of a campaign to bring about international talks on combating terrorism. Presumably a major Soviet motivation was the desire to cleanse Moscow's reputation and demonstrate its new policies. Taken in conjunction with the above reports of actual cooperation, however, the new Soviet proposals may not have been entirely propaganda-oriented. The campaign began with a proposal by the Soviet delegation to the Conference on Security and Cooperation in Europe (CSCE) talks in Vienna in February 1987, in which the Soviets termed all acts of terrorism "criminal" regardless of their perpetrators.[43] The Soviets also approached individual West European governments with this idea and with suggestions for negotiating extradition agreements.[44] The proposal, which was brought to the UN General Assembly in the summer of 1987, called for international endorsement of a number of principles on the subject. The suggestion to the United Nations, however, was quite general, with at least implied criticism of Western use of force; it recognized the legitimacy of the struggle of national liberation movements and condemned the use of force and international terrorism regardless of its source.[45]

At the same time, Soviet authorities reportedly asked to be included in Western efforts to curb terrorism, complaining when they were not invited to a European Community (EC) meeting on the topic with North Americans and Japanese.[46] As usual, the Soviets did attend the annual International Civil Aviation Organization conference in Montreal in February. They sent a large, high-level delegation that, according to TASS, was well received because of the Soviet decision to adhere to the Tokyo Convention on Offenses and Certain Other Acts Committed on Board Aircraft.[47]

From January 23 to 27, 1989, the Soviets held their own international conference on counterterrorism. Although it was sponsored by *Literaturnaia gazeta* rather than by a governmental body, it was attended by a number of mid-level government officials and opened with an official greeting by the deputy head of the Soviet Foreign Ministry's legal department. Participating on the Soviet side, in addition to this Foreign Ministry official and journalists from the sponsoring newspaper, were Interior Ministry official Evgenii Liakhov and legal expert Lidiia Modzhorian (both of whom generally dealt with international terrorism and aviation security), as well as academics and researchers, including Gleb Starushenko (who normally dealt with international law and national liberation movements), and specialists on the Middle East, Africa, and the Third World in general. Presumably to downplay any official character of the meeting or perhaps to protect the involvement of some with the issue of terrorism, Soviet reporting of the conference mentioned only six participants from each side and omitted any reference to the Soviet officials present (with the exception of Ljahov, who was described only by his academic titles).[48]

That the Soviets intended the conference to serve more than propaganda purposes was suggested by the invitation of serious Western experts on terrorism, including some not noted for their favorable attitude toward Soviet involvement and many who serve as consultants to the U.S. government. Moreover, the conference was agreed by both U.S. and Soviet participants to be part of an ongoing cooperative project called by the Americans "The U.S.-Soviet Task Force for the Prevention of Terrorism." The Soviets called this a "Soviet-American Society for Jointly Fighting International Terrorism," thus downplaying again any official involvement and explicitly opening up the conference to representatives of other countries. After a number of meetings, the two delegations did decide to produce a joint book and to present their findings and recommendations to their respective governments. Igor Beliaev, senior *Literaturnaia gazeta* commentator and Middle East expert, and Latin American expert Sergei Mikoian were the Soviet initiators of the project, organized jointly between *Literaturnaia gazeta* and the Washington-based group "Search for Common

Understanding." The proposed volume, which would include recommendations for preventing and dealing with terrorism, would be published simultaneously in the Soviet Union and the United States.[49]

At this first conference of the task force, the Soviet participants reportedly described their major concern about terrorism: the possibility that a terrorist incident could provoke a conflict resulting in a nuclear clash. The scenario might include U.S. action against a Soviet client that Moscow might feel obliged to defend. Invoking Gorbachev's connection of terrorism with regional conflicts, the Soviets expressed their fear that terrorism could lead to wider conflict, as had already occurred in the Middle East. The Soviets reportedly were also afraid that the terrorist methods of Islamic fundamentalists in the Middle East could spread to the Soviet Union's own Moslem population or ethnic minorities. Still another Soviet concern was the possible terrorist use of chemical, biological, or nuclear weapons. It was also a source of Soviet concern that the Soviet Union has been an increasingly frequent victim of terrorism in recent years.

Conference participants were able to reach agreement on at least a working definition of terrorism without tackling the issue of the use of violence by national liberation or other movements supported by either the Soviet Union or the United States. This definition, proposed by a participant from the Soviet Ministry of Interior, was as follows:

> International terrorism represents the sum total of the following activities:
>
> a) illegal and premeditated acts of violence committed by people (or by a group of people) on the territory of a state directed toward foreign nationals or international organs or institutions, or toward personnel [Soviet version said "their personnel"], means of international transportation or communication, and other foreign or international objects;

b) illegal or premeditated acts of violence committed by people (or groups of people) organized or supported by a foreign state on a given state's territory directed toward national state organs or public institutions, national political or public figures, populations or other objects. [Soviet version added here: "The goal of terrorism is to obtain privileges or advantages illegally from a larger group of people against whom the terrorism is immediately directed."][50]

It was agreed that some acts should be universally prohibited — for example, attacks on civil aviation (either sabotage or hijackings), attacks on internationally protected individuals (such as children or diplomats), and attacks on ships or sea platforms or the mining of sea lanes. Beyond this, the participants agreed upon the following recommendations, which they apparently intended to present to their respective governments:

1. Creation of a standing bilateral group and channel of communications for exchange of information on terrorism — in effect, a designated link for conveying requests and relaying information during a terrorist crisis.

2. Provision of mutual assistance (information, diplomatic assistance, technical assistance, and so forth) in the investigation of terrorist incidents.

3. Prohibition of the sale or transfer of military explosives and certain classes of weapons (such as surface to air missiles) to non-governmental organizations, and increased controls on the sale or transfer to governments.

4. Initiation of bilateral discussions on requiring chemical or other types of "tags" in commercial and military explosives to make them more easily detectable and to aid in the investigation of terrorist bombings.

5. Initiation of joint efforts to prevent terrorists from acquiring chemical, biological, nuclear, or other means of mass destruction.

6. Exchange of anti-terrorist technology, consis-

tent with the national security interests as defined by
each nation.

7. Conduct of joint exercises and simulations in or-
der to develop further means of Soviet-American cooperation during terrorist threats or incidents.

8. Joint action to fill the gaps that exist in current
international law and institutions, including the establishment of a United Nations Standing Committee on
International Terrorism.[51]

Even if they were unofficial, the very convocation of
this conference and the creation of the joint task force were
significant events in themselves. Still more significant were
the above recommendations, particularly because many of
the Soviet participants were directly involved in the definition and even treatment of terrorism—although not necessarily directly responsible for Soviet relations with groups
that practice terrorism.[52] If Moscow actually were to adopt
these recommendations (for example, the proposal to prevent the supply of SA-7s to "non-governmental groups," a
category that clearly included national liberation movements), it would definitely be a reversal of its policy up to
now.

Without in any way belittling the importance of this
joint venture (itself mentioned by TASS), it should be noted
that Soviet treatment of the conference and the group was
somewhat different from the U.S. approach. The only comprehensive Soviet report of the event, which was published
by the host *Literaturnaia gazeta* some six weeks later, emphasized the constructive and congenial atmosphere, the
possibility of U.S.-Soviet cooperation, and the changes that
had made the event possible.[53] It had somewhat less to say
about the content itself. (Starushenko also noted the extraordinary nature of the event, but he alone appeared to
take the old approach with his claim—reported by the Soviets but not by the Americans—that the Soviets had always
opposed terrorism, the only change being U.S. willingness
finally to acknowledge their position.) The Soviet account

devoted a good deal of attention to formal international organs, particularly the United Nations, as the appropriate vehicles for action. It mentioned the agreed-upon recommendations only as comments made by various U.S. speakers. It may be that the Soviets truly were more impressed by their own ability to meet with such respected U.S. experts without resorting to propaganda attacks and polemics; the fact of *perestroika* may have been of greater interest to them than actual results at the present time. Yet one is also struck by their greater cautiousness and more limited aspirations compared with the Americans, at least in public. Presumably this reaction was at least partly the result of Soviet sensitivity for the movements and causes the Soviet Union ostensibly supports. It may also be partly due to concern about those who still oppose the policy changes under way.

5

Soviet Policy toward Groups That Use Terrorism

The new approach of international cooperation in combating terrorism was part of Gorbachev's overall revamping of Soviet foreign policy. As part of his proclaimed effort to end regional conflicts, it also involved a new approach to armed struggle. There were a number of examples of the application of the new policy, including Soviet behavior in the Middle East. Moscow's preference for a political resolution of the Arab-Israeli conflict led to the Soviet initiation of an improvement in Soviet relations with Israel, as well as with a number of pro-Western Arab states. Although such a policy provoked objections from Moscow's more radical ally, Syria, it was apparently perceived in the Kremlin as an expedient and effective way to resolve the Arab-Israeli conflict and achieve regional stability. Similar steps toward Saudi Arabia in connection with the Afghan conflict, and even toward South Africa in connection with the Angolan conflict, were some indication of the new approach. (They were also part of Moscow's more open, pragmatic approach to conservative or capitalist states in the Third World, as dictated by the new thinking.) Even in Central America, the quest for political resolution of conflict became apparent in Soviet behavior. It remains to be seen, however, if these changes, together with the altered Soviet approach to terrorism under Gorbachev, have changed actual Soviet behavior toward the movements and groups that use terrorism.

Aid and Advice

Has Moscow in fact altered or terminated its support (advice, arms supplies, training, and logistics) for would-be terrorists? This question is difficult to answer. One delicate issue—Soviet arms supplies and their connection with terrorism—has been critically if tentatively raised in unpublished and published discussions in the Soviet Union. Kozyrev and Primakov, as well as others, obliquely referred only to the past role of the Soviet Union in the militarization of Third World conflicts. Africa Institute director Anatoli Gromyko may have implied slightly more when, in a published dialogue with visiting U.S. scholars, he called for the Soviet Union and the United States to discuss an end to the "flow of arms" into the Third World, "where most of the regional conflicts occur."[1]

The Foreign Ministry–*Mezhdunarodnaia zhizn'* symposium late in 1988 went much further, devoting a good deal of attention to the Soviet Union's contribution to the arms race in the Third World.[2] Deputy head of the Africa Institute Alexeii Vasilyev, along with Oleg Peresypkin, rector of the Foreign Ministry's Diplomacy Institute, and Viktor Kremeniuk, all called for a cutback in Soviet arms deliveries to conflict areas, belittling the amount of political influence that could be gained by such deliveries. Peresypkin called on the Soviet Union to "discard [the] double moral standards" that enabled it to speak of resolving conflicts while continuing to supply arms. Presumably, the deliveries included supplies to movements as well as states. The only one to make a more direct connection and thereby touch upon even an indirect Soviet role in international terrorism, however, was a more junior journalist, Galina Sidorova. Writing in the *New Times*, she called for a ban on arms trafficking (or at least a resumption of U.S.-Soviet talks on the issue) on the grounds that "the arms sold break away from the seller and often follow their own, extremely unpredictable course."[3] At the U.S.-Soviet conference on terrorism, Andrei Shumikhin of the USA-Canada Institute also spoke of the need to cut back arms deliveries; because the subject of this conference was terrorism, he was clearly referring to the supplies provided movements and groups using terrorism, although he did not say so directly.[4]

The matter of Soviet arms supplies to nongovernmental groups abroad has rarely been mentioned. Military aid to some anticolonial liberation movements was occasionally but only rarely mentioned in Soviet media, and such aid in the past (to separatists such as the Iraqi Kurds, for example) has been referred to only once or twice in historical accounts. If Soviet arms were used for less honorable purposes (that is, for movements employing terrorism), the subject has obviously been taboo. Sidorova's comments, and to a lesser degree Shumikhin's, are therefore perhaps the most direct published reference to date. If this essential element of Soviet involvement were to be addressed at any level, it would indicate significant progress in a changing Soviet position.

It has been virtually impossible to determine, however, if Soviet arms supplies (never very significant except to the PLO), have in fact been curtailed. Soviet arms have remained the terrorists' weapons of choice, including the Czechoslovak SAMTEX explosives linked as recently as December 1988 to the bombing of the Pan Am plane over Scotland, apparently by operatives of Ahmad Jibril's splinter group, the rejectionist Popular Front for the Liberation of Palestine–General Command (PFLP-GC). Yet the presence of such equipment has never firmly indicated direct Soviet bloc supplies, particularly when splinter groups were involved. In fact, there have been rumors that the PLO itself has been having difficulty obtaining Soviet arms. Inasmuch as Palestinian complaints about Soviet arms supplies are not new, however, the exact meaning of the problem remains unclear. There had been a break in Soviet training and direct arms supplies to Fatah during the Arafat-Hussein agreement in 1985 and part of 1986. East European aid reportedly had continued, as had Soviet assistance to the other PLO factions, specifically the PFLP of George Habash and the Democratic Front for the Liberation of Palestine (DFLP) of Nayif Hawatmeh. Moscow did resume training of Fatah personnel and presumably arms supplies following the Soviet-mediated reunification of the PLO in April 1987.

There were also some in the Soviet media who appeared to support the idea of Palestinian terrorism, possibly even that of Ahmad Jibril's PFLP-GC. Konstantin Geivandov, *Izvestiia*'s Middle East expert and a senior commentator for the paper, wrote in admiring tones of his meetings with PLO operatives during a visit to the Middle East, including a meeting with PFLP-GC's Talal Naji. Geivandov described Naji as deputy general secretary of the PFLP-GC, the members of which "carried out the daring hang glider raid on an Israeli military base" in 1987. He praised this raid as having had "an enormous impact."[5] A few months earlier, in November 1987, *Pravda* had delivered a long defense of the PLO, justifying its use of armed struggle while denying its use of terrorism.[6] In the same vein, an official of the news agency Novosti was quoted in Kuwait in June 1988 as defending the PLO's use of armed struggle within the occupied territories, and this position could also be found in *Izvestiia*'s justification of the killing of an Israeli military policeman in Gaza in August 1987.[7] None of these positive remarks condoned or even referred to attacks on civilians and, therefore, could not technically be accused of supporting terrorism. Yet there was quite a fine line between "armed struggle" and terrorism when dealing with PLO actions inside Israel, especially when speaking of operations conducted by Ahmad Jibril's organization.

In contrast, the bombing of a Pan Am plane in December 1988, which is believed to have been carried out by Jibril's organization, was criticized by the Soviet media. Seeking to obfuscate any Palestinian connection with the operation, however, the Soviet press reported an offer by the PLO to assist in the search for the guilty parties. More directly, as noted earlier, at least two admittedly Palestinian attacks, one on new recruits in Jerusalem and one on a civilian bus in the occupied territories, were actually referred to as "terrorist" actions by Soviet media. The bus attack even elicited a condemnation by Soviet Foreign Ministry spokesman Gennadii Gerasimov of terrorism "no matter where and no matter by whom."[8]

In the same vein, two articles in the *New Times* spoke of the PLO's vacillation between what one commentator called "a war of liberation and peaceful means of attaining the ultimate goal."[9] The second commentator, historian Leonid Medvedko, wrote about the convergence of "extremists" on both sides, noting the futility of "terrorism, individual, group or state," and condemning violence as "sterile."[10] Medvedko's recommendations as to means were particularly significant, for he addressed the disagreement within the Palestinian camp as well as the Arab world about this issue. Both journalists commented on Arafat's past preference for armed struggle "and other forms of violence," but the implication, particularly of Medvedko, was that Arafat had now changed his position. He nonetheless concluded that the lack of control over extremists (in the Arab and Palestinian camp) might prevent the necessary conversion of the stone throwing by the *intifada* to a "collect[ion] of stones" for a peaceful settlement. The first of these articles was published during Arafat's visit to Moscow in April 1988; a second, much more explicitly critical article, was published at the time of Habash's September visit to Moscow, in what was part of Soviet consultations with Hawatmeh and a PLO executive delegation before the November 1988 meeting of the Palestine National Council (PNC).

Indeed, just after these visits, *Sovetskaia rossiya* carried a very unusual article by Rami as-Shaer, whom it described as a "PLO publicist." As-Shaer was in fact a Palestinian who had once been the PLO official representative in Moscow, but had remained in the Soviet Union after his replacement; he was considered actually to be closer to Moscow than to the PLO. In his article, as-Shaer was probably expressing Soviet opinions, urging the PNC to adopt measures "which would have nothing in common with extremism" and would convince the next U.S. administration of the need to deal with the Palestinians.[11] Quoting PLO leader Salah Khalaf (Abu Iyyad) on the presence of extremists in the Palestinian movement, as-Shaer warned against giving them an opportunity "to dictate their will to the entire movement" or to set the tone for future actions. He also praised the PLO for placing its emphasis on unarmed struggle in the territories, "despite calls from radical forces in the Arab world" and despite the Palestinian right to any method of struggle.

The message being conveyed to the PLO was indeed one against the use of armed struggle, and it was suggested in Shevardnadze's speech honoring Arafat during Arafat's April 1988 visit. The Soviet foreign minister said that "the new political thinking must become here [in the Near East], as everywhere, the main direction of policy. *In other words, if you must arm yourself, then it should only be with the political means of a peaceful settlement of disputed problems*, with absolute respect for equality and equal security, and respect for the right to self-determination, independence, sovereignty and the territorial integrity of every state and people."[12] Shevardnadze's choice of words strongly suggested that Moscow's advice was being backed up by concrete restraints in the area of arms deliveries. The advice was apparently repeated in the talks between Soviet and PLO leaders before the November PNC meeting, during which Moscow sought to persuade the PLO and, in particular, to convince the PFLP and DFLP to favor a moderate position—that is, a political solution. For this reason, the PNC's decision in November 1988 and Arafat's subsequent renunciations of terrorism in all forms resulted in no small part from Moscow's pressures.

It is likely then that the continuing attempts by Palestinian dissidents, and even by the PFLP and DFLP, to send terrorists across Israel's borders have not been assisted by Moscow. The Soviet media have critically pointed out the existence of opposition within the PLO to Arafat's renunciation of terrorism and his call for a political settlement, mentioning that this opposition is supported by Syria, Libya, and Iran. Fatah rebel Abu Musa was described as the "leader of the militant radicals" who were calling for armed struggle against Israel, while the PFLP and DFLP were mildly chastized for deviating from their earlier acceptance, according to *Izvestiia*, of the PNC decisions.[13] With regard to the attempted incursions themselves, *Izvestiia* quoted Israeli Chief of Staff Dan Shomron to the effect that the PLO had not carried out any attacks against Israel since November, adding Shomron's comment that this did not include the "rejection front," which accounted for what was said to be increased infiltration attempts by individual armed Arabs. Egyptian President Hosni Mubarak was quoted more directly denying PLO involvement in the terrorist attempts.[14]

Soviet pressures may have had some effect even before the PNC renunciations of terrorism. International terrorist actions conducted by the PLO, particularly by Arafat's own Fatah, declined after 1986.[15] Only 17 percent of international terrorist attacks in 1987 were conducted by Palestinians. Of these, 21 incidents (51 percent) were conducted by Abu Nidal's faction, 4 by Black September (also believed to be linked to Abu Nidal's group), 4 by the dissident Palestinian May-15 group, 2 by Fatah rebels under Abu Musa, and 3 by Fatah itself.[16] Attacks by Abu Nidal have also declined over the past two years, reportedly because of an agreement with Fatah but possibly also because of Soviet withdrawal of indirect support.[17]

In January 1988, the Polish government announced that it had expelled a Palestinian businessman connected with Abu Nidal and ceased the operations, some six months before, of a trading company claimed by the United States to have been a front in Poland for assisting Abu Nidal. East Germany took similar steps. During the spring of 1987, Abu Nidal's training camps in Syria were closed, as was his office in Damascus in June, possibly the result of Soviet pressures as well as Western sanctions.[18] A *New Times* article in 1989 praised the PLO, specifically Fatah, for abandoning the use of terrorism and singled out Abu Nidal for strong, detailed condemnation.[19] Nonetheless, this group has been linked to a number of attempts in early 1989 to infiltrate Israel from Syrian-held parts of Lebanon. The article may have had this in mind when it referred to the support provided to the Abu Nidal group by "certain Arab politicians who favour extremist methods of resolving the Middle East question."

Libya presumably fell into the same category. According to the *New York Times*, several Western governments urged the Soviet Union in 1987 to try to curb Libya's support for terrorism. Moscow may have tried to comply in talks with Libyan leader A. S. Jallud held in Moscow in May 1986. The communiqué published in *Pravda* at the close of the visit contained what could be interpreted as implied criticism of Libyan support for international terrorism. Its statement about crisis situations that "serve imperialist circles for the escalation of international tension and intervention in the internal affairs of sovereign states" clearly referred to the U.S. action against Libya in 1985.[20] In January 1989, a *Literaturnaia gazeta* article noted that Soviet "colleagues" often shared Western impressions of Qadhafi as "a nationalist, Islamic fanatic, terrorist, and anti-Communist."[21] Whether this reflected outside pressures or views expressed by the Soviet leadership in conversations with the Libyans is difficult to determine.

TASS reported a Libyan condemnation of the wave of terrorist attacks that hit France in September 1986 — attacks alleged to have been linked with Libya — and quoted the Libyan representative in Paris as expressing willingness to cooperate in international efforts to eliminate terrorism.[22] Officially, however, the most Moscow could get out of Libya publicly was a joint communiqué in June 1987 that called for an "international conference under the auspices of the UN to define terrorism and distinguish between it and the national liberation struggle of various peoples."[23] Nonetheless, terrorist incidents traceable to Libya declined in 1987 as compared with 1986 – possibly as a result of Soviet pressure. Indeed, both Libya and Syria became significantly less active in international terrorism during 1986–1987.[24]

In the case of Syria, exactly the same proposal for a conference, with the same wording, was included in the communiqué at the close of President Hafiz al-Asad's visit in April 1987. The Soviets were also able to get Syria to add a condemnation of terrorism "of all types . . . carried out by individuals, groups or governments" as a serious threat to "peace, security and international cooperation."[25] This was the formulation used in the communiqué with a visiting PLO delegation in June as well, which, interestingly, did not add any exception for national liberation struggles. Nor did the condemnation of terrorism included in the communiqué at the close of Shevardnadze's February 1989 visit to Damascus include such an exemption, although it did call for an international conference that would "work out a generally acceptable definition of terrorism."[26]

The need for a definition of terrorism may have been a concession to the claim by some (presumably Syria) that armed struggle conducted by a national liberation movement could not be considered terrorism, no matter what form it took. Yet a few weeks earlier Gleb Starushenko, the leading Soviet expert in international law and a frequent champion of national liberation movements and their right to armed struggle, expressed what may have been a new dissociation. Arguing that all hijackings should be considered international terrorism, he claimed that one reason the struggle against hijackings was not sufficiently effective was because "some states equate international terrorism with liberation movements and evade carrying out their international obligations."[27] Nonetheless, the call in the Soviet-Syrian communiqué for Syria to convene an antiterrorism conference appeared cynical at the least, given that Syria was then backing attempts by dissident Palestinians to launch terrorist attacks inside Israel (as admitted in at least one Soviet paper).[28] Including the issue of terrorism at this time, however, may indicate that Shevardnadze raised the matter with Asad.

Relations with Movements and Groups

It is not entirely clear that these public positions and pressures at the highest official levels are fully reflected in or respected by the lower level of KGB operatives or the local Communist parties. The Lebanese Communist Party, for example, has been involved in numerous terrorist incidents in Lebanon, including the attempted assassination of the commander of the South Lebanese Forces in 1988.[29] Thus, when the factional fighting in Lebanon involved attacks on these South Lebanese Christians, the operations were described as "guerrilla warfare by Lebanese patriots engaged in armed struggle for the liberation of their homeland."[30] The killing of members of the Lebanese Communist Party, however, were termed terrorist acts.[31] The distinction could be justified because the first acts were against armed forces, while the second were against civilians. Yet the pattern was clear, and the involvement of Lebanese Communists in interfactional acts of violence, including car bombs and other clearly terrorist actions, strongly suggested, if not Soviet approval, then an exceedingly serious lack of Soviet control over a party closely tied to Moscow. The Soviet Union has been opposed to (and a victim of) the Iranian-sponsored Hizballah-Islamic Jihad organization and has labeled its actions "terrorist."[32] Yet there were reports in 1983 and 1984 of some Soviet support for the rival Islamic Amal in Lebanon. It is not clear if this support, reportedly in the form of arms and training, has continued.[33]

Like the PLO, the case of the South African ANC, another movement traditionally supported by Moscow, offers some evidence of changes under Gorbachev.[34] In the early period of the Gorbachev regime, Soviet articles appeared to parallel the more radical decisions adopted by the ANC Congress of June 1985. One journal quoted an ANC official on the inevitability of a "people's war" in South Africa, while others spoke of a "revolutionary situation" in the country, implying the appropriateness of a stepped-up armed struggle.[35] As late as 1987, a SWAPO official, writing in the *World Marxist Review*, praised the armed struggle carried out by the ANC in South Africa, attributing progress primarily to the "combat operations conducted by the military wing of the ANC."[36] But for this one exception, however, one would be hard-pressed to find similar statements by a Soviet source or even an ANC official in a Soviet publication after 1986. Soviet experts themselves point to the change in the Soviet approach to the South African problem, dating it to the mid-1980s.[37]

The first public signs of this change became apparent with and immediately following Gorbachev's speech to the CPSU Congress in February 1986. The new Soviet leader dedicated only a small part of a sentence to the area when he called for "a collective search for ways to solve the conflict situations" in the Middle East, Central America, and southern Africa.[38] The following month, in a speech honoring the visit of Mozambique's President Samora Machel, Gorbachev clearly indicated that his call for *political* resolution of regional conflicts applied to the conflict within South Africa. Gorbachev made his point again, more explicitly, in speeches in April and August 1987 honoring British Prime Minister Margaret Thatcher and Mozambique's new President Joaquím Chissano, respectively.[39] These were accompanied by articles warning against indiscriminate violence, even if the ANC's choice of armed struggle was deemed understandable.[40]

According to South African expert Philip Nel, the ANC and the Communist Party of South Africa also gradually accepted this distinction "between legitimate armed struggle and excessive and indiscriminate violence" (perhaps because much of the worst violence was being conducted spontaneously by radical youngsters, some identified with the rival liberation organization, the Pan-Africanist Congress or PAC).[41] Thus, senior Soviet Africanist Boris Asoyan (deputy head of the Foreign Ministry's African Department) graphically described, and condemned, some of the atrocities committed by violent extremist black nationalists in South Africa and warned about "rampant violence throwing revolutions off the revolutionary path."[42] He quoted a Nelson Mandela statement of 25 years ago against "outbreaks of terrorism." Asoyan went on to speak of revolution in South Africa as a long process that required most of all the strengthening of the revolutionary classes.

Similarly, a South African journalist, presumably a Communist, described some of the methods being used and planned for use in this process. In an article in the *World Marxist Review*, he wrote at some length about passive resistance and civil disobedience, noting ANC and Communist denunciation of acts of brutality.[43] Although he mentioned the "combat actions of the people's army," he singled out "organization" as "the key to [their] victory." Soviet Africanist V. N. Tetiokin wrote that a new stage, one of grassroots political work, had been reached in South Africa, while TASS political analyst Sergei Kulik explained that under present conditions (a heavily armed South Africa) "the continuation of a military conflict in which there can be no winners in fact amounts to mutual destruction."[44] Referring to both the Namibian and the antiapartheid struggle, he ruled out liberation war, urging "realism" and "stage-by-stage normalization" as well as armed struggle. According to ANC officials, this same message was forcefully conveyed to them in talks with the Soviets, and, they claimed, pressures upon the ANC to approach the negotiating table were even stronger from Moscow than from the West.[45]

As in the case of the PLO, it is difficult to know if the advice being given the ANC reflected actual changes in aid and training, for example. Given the importance of South Africa in progressive Western circles as well as in the Third World, and the increased status accorded the ANC as late as the fall of 1987 (when an ANC office with diplomatic status was opened in Moscow), it seems unlikely that there would be a significant change in aid policy. In fact, ANC leader Oliver Tambo reportedly received promises of increased Soviet military aid from the Soviet leadership during a visit to Moscow in November 1986. Soviet military aid to the ANC had never been very large, however, even compared with supplies to other movements. The figure revealed in 1986 by an ANC official was $50 million annually, less than that rendered to ZAPU during its struggle in Zimbabwe during the 1970s or to SWAPO during the past 10 years.[46] In the summer of 1987, following the seizure of an arms cache by Pretoria police, the ANC acknowledged that it had received military assistance from the Soviet bloc.[47] There have been no reports or even rumors of any reduction in arms supplies, training, or other assistance rendered the ANC by the Soviet Union or Soviet bloc countries.

In Namibia, SWAPO was engaged for years in an armed struggle, without significant use of terrorism. The Soviets supported this struggle through arms supplies and training, even as it urged a political solution. This position did not appear to have changed under Gorbachev. Indeed, a *New Times* article in August 1988 spoke of the legitimacy of SWAPO's armed struggle and warned that this struggle would be augmented if the effort to find a political solution through the Angolan peace talks failed.[48] Nonetheless, in May 1988, Deputy Foreign Minister Anatolii Adamishin clearly stated that the Soviet Union wanted a political solution for the southern African situation and welcomed what he called the emergence of a political settlement in the U.S.-sponsored talks.[49] The Soviets encouraged and assisted in these talks, including a certain degree of persuasion with regard to their Cuban allies. In this respect, the search for an end to regional conflicts characteristic of the new thinking was at play. The successful conclusion of the negotiations, with the agreement on Namibian independence, removed the need for any Soviet decision regarding SWAPO or the continued support of its armed struggle.

The Soviet position toward the struggle of the Polisario appears to be much the same, although Moscow has given the Polisario much less direct support over the years than it has given the purely anticolonial Namibian movement. Moreover, most of the support for the armed struggle had been indirect, mainly through Algeria. Even this support was sometimes conducted with only Soviet approval, not as a result of a Soviet initiative. This presumably was because of sensitivity to interests, particularly economic, regarding Morocco. Therefore, Soviet recommendations for a political settlement, in the form of negotiations and a referendum, are not new. As in the case of SWAPO, however, there appears to be Soviet pressure to reach a compromise through UN mediation.[50] Soviet mediation of some type was evident from talks with a personal representative of King Hassan II of Morocco in Moscow in September 1988; this representative was said to have conveyed to the Soviets his position regarding a settlement to the conflict.[51] There is reason to believe that this message was, in fact, solicited by Moscow in an effort to bring about an end to this conflict as well.

There have been no indications whether Soviet support and aid for groups such as the Kurds or the Armenians in Turkey have undergone any changes. Earlier Turkish Communist reticence toward the radical Turkish Kurds' Workers Party (PKK) had given way to support in the early 1980s. Signs of this support could be found, albeit sparingly, in Soviet media, including an article in 1985 critical of Turkish treatment of its Kurds. As late as 1986 there were Turkish government reports of Soviet training of the PKK in Syria.[52] Palestinian assistance was also available, with or without Soviet involvement. In the same year an official of the Turkish Armenian group, ASALA, revealed that the Soviets were assisting this group by means of arms supplies and training. The same official, however, bemoaned the fact that Moscow did not permit cooperation with or use of Soviet Armenia for this purpose.[53] Here, too, Syria as well as the PLO (Fatah and the PFLP) appear to have been helpful, either independently or at the behest of the Soviets.

There may have been a change in the Soviet attitude toward the rebellion in southern Sudan. Although there was little enthusiasm for this separatist movement before Gorbachev, the fact that it was aided by Moscow's ally Ethiopia had led to some Soviet support, particularly in periods of strain in Moscow's relationship with Sudanese President Ga'far Numieri. It was never clear if this actually included arms and training from Moscow or if, as in the case of the Polisario, Moscow merely acquiesced to the requests of the neighboring regime, in this case Addis Ababa. The movement itself claimed late in 1985 that it had no contact with Moscow. In any case, Soviet references in 1988 to "terrorist" attacks in the Sudanese city of Khartoum, carried out presumably by the Sudan Peoples' Liberation Movement (SPLM), suggest that the Soviets and possibly the Ethiopians themselves were no longer willing to support this movement.[54] This might account in part for the opening of negotiations in 1988 to settle this conflict.

A case in which the change has been much more certain and dramatic is that of the Tamils in Sri Lanka. Here, too, support had been indirect – through (and presumably because of) India. In 1987, the Soviet media began openly and strongly to condemn the Tamils' use of force, dedicating some of its strongest language against terrorism to condemning the Tamils. With this reversal, Moscow probably ended whatever material support it had been supplying, directly or indirectly. The reversal itself, however, was not necessarily a result of the new thinking. Rather, the Soviets were reverting to their earlier opposition to the separatist Tamils – an opposition only suspended when India supported the movement. In 1987, when Indian peacekeeping forces in Sri Lanka began themselves to battle the Tamils, Moscow changed its position and began condemning Tamil terrorism again, now in much stronger terms. Other terrorist activity in Sri Lanka, by radicals in the south, appears to be Maoist in orientation and unconnected to Moscow.[55]

There are some signs, though very slight, that the Soviets may have changed their attitude toward the IRA. Evidence of direct Soviet support had never been entirely clear, and Moscow had expressed opposition to terrorism in Northern Ireland in the past, even as evidence of arms supplies became clearer. In 1988, however, Soviet media digressed from their usually noncommittal reporting of violence in Northern Ireland to characterize an IRA action as "barbaric."[56] In an interview in Ulster with a Soviet journalist, James Stewart, head of the Communist Party of Ireland, rejected the "method of armed struggle" waged by the Provisional IRA on the grounds that it was counterproductive.[57] Another Soviet article bemoaned the presence of "violence, terrorism, and extremism" in Northern Ireland. But such minor signs of condemnation had appeared even in the pre-Gorbachev period. Surprising reports in early February 1989 of the opening of albeit short-lived talks in Ulster may have indicated that the wave of reconciliation apparent elsewhere in the world was approaching Ireland as well. One would have to concede a great deal more Soviet involvement to draw a connection between these phenomena, however. The threat that Soviet arms would no longer be readily available might be a factor, but past connections are so tenuous as to defy even this conclusion.

The same reasoning may be applied with regard to the Basque movement in Spain. No firm evidence has ever been provided in the past for direct Soviet support or involvement with this movement. Both Soviet reticence about supporting separatist movements and the general absence of direct Soviet involvement with movements in Western Europe presumably accounted for this. Yet the agreement of the Basques to a cease-fire and the opening of talks in Algeria early in 1989, at the same time that Moscow was guiding other movements toward political settlement, suggested a probable connection. Also it seemed significant that Algeria was chosen as the venue for the talks, given Algeria's former role as trainer and supplier of many Soviet-supported movements. These connections, however, were highly tenuous; any conclusions are therefore purely speculative.

In Latin America, there are also tenuous signs that the

Soviet Union no longer wishes to support armed struggle —
for example, in El Salvador. As with Ireland, these signs are
based more in rhetoric than on fact, although there have
been rumors that Nicaragua has withheld certain arms supplies (apparently SA-7s) to the Salvadorian rebels, possibly
at the behest of the Soviets. Nonetheless, an article in the
New Times in October 1988 said that the Left in El Salvador favored armed struggle but that "75 per cent of the
population favour a negotiated settlement."[58] This information was said to explain the victory of the right-wing Nationalist Republican Alliance in the 1988 elections. The article by no means criticized armed struggle, however, even as
it remarked positively that the Left was also conducting a
parliamentary struggle. Ilya Prizel, a Western specialist on
Latin America, has claimed that although the Soviets have
not been involved in any significant arms transfers to the
Salvadorian guerrillas, some Soviet specialists apparently
continue to believe that armed struggle in El Salvador can
succeed.[59]

As noted earlier, the July 1988 issue of the *World Marxist Review* carried a discussion with Latin American Communists in which the path of democratic reform was advocated, particularly by the Soviet representative. If this was
meant to represent actual policy, it would probably be a
relatively recent Soviet decision. As late as 1986, the government of General Augusto Pinochet in Chile declared
that it had intercepted 10 tons of arms supplies transported
by Soviet trawlers destined for Chilean terrorists.[60] In September 1986, the Patriotic Front, created in part by Communists in 1983 and often associated with the illegal Communist Party, attempted to assassinate Pinochet. Since
1980, the Communist Party of Chile had indeed adopted a
policy of employing "all means," including terrorism, although there were differing views within the party on this
issue.

The clandestine party congress, held intermittently
throughout the spring of 1989, was reported to be reconsid-
ering its use of violence. The debate itself was presumably

prompted by the recent referendum in Chile that went against Pinochet and paved the way for elections scheduled for December 1989. Although illegal today, the Communist Party must decide whether to participate—that is, whether to employ peaceful, parliamentary means, perhaps through the legal, newly formed Party of the Socialist Left, which includes a number of Communists. It is possible, as the comments reported in the *World Marxist Review* suggest, that officials in Moscow have urged the Chilean Communists to reconsider their violent tactics in view of the changes in Soviet policy.

Nonetheless, the document prepared for the congress repeated the by now standard appraisal that the failure of the Salvador Allende experiment in Chile was due to the unwillingness of the party to use force to defend the revolution, invoking the Cuban example of the need to fight militarily. Moreover, a leading Communist Party ideologist Volodia Tietelboim said upon his return from a four-month visit to the Soviet Union that the party would continue to employ "all forms of struggle."[61] It is far from clear if this statement had Moscow's support, particularly in view of the fact that the Chilean party has the reputation of being unsympathetic to Gorbachev's reforms. In addition, other Communist spokesmen in Chile have indeed argued against the use of violence. Just what Moscow has advised can only be guessed, as the Chilean party undergoes this internal dispute over the tactics to be employed.

As for other parties or movements in Latin America, there were reports in 1987 that the Soviets, as well as Cubans and Libyans, were training and supplying such Mexican groups as the LC-23.[62] No information is available on today's relationship (if any) between Moscow and the radical groups most active in their use of terror: the Peruvian Movimiento Revolucionaria de Tupac Amaru (MRTA), Sendero Luminoso (SL), and the Colombian Ejercito de Liberacion Nacional (ELN). There had been reports in the early 1980s of Soviet (as well as Cuban and Libyan) training of the Colombian M-19 movement; this movement's actions declined significantly in 1987.[63] Whether this was connected with Soviet advice, supplies, or other signs from Moscow is not known.

New Involvements

Of particular interest are new connections or increased activities since Gorbachev's ascent. With the rise in nationalist activity in New Caledonia, there has been open Soviet support for independence there. It is not clear, however, if this political propaganda support has been accompanied by material assistance (training, arms, and logistics). There was a report as early as 1984 that the leader of the Kanak Socialist National Liberation Front (FLNK) in New Caledonia approached the Soviet Union for such aid. Australia expressed concern about the emerging relationship between the South Pacific Islands and Libya, as well as about alleged arms smuggling to the area and the dispatching of islanders to Libya for what is believed to be training purposes.[64] In the past, Libya has assisted movements ignored and even opposed by Moscow, but signs of growing Soviet commercial and political involvement with the South Pacific Islands over the past three years suggest at least a Soviet interest in, if not actual aid to, the Kanaks of New Caledonia. Canberra has also complained about Libyan assistance to aboriginal dissidents in Australia, but no Soviet role has been mentioned.[65]

A movement previously assisted by Libya (and the PLO), even when opposed by the Soviets, was the traditionally pro-Chinese Communist National People's Army (NPA) and their sometime allies—the Moro National Liberation Front—in the Philippines. Stepped-up guerrilla and terrorist activities by both groups in 1986 and 1987 (they declined in 1988) were accompanied by rumors of Soviet bloc assistance.[66] In January 1987, two prominent Filipino leaders of the Maoist Communist Party of the Philippines asserted that Moscow had offered "unlimited arms and funds" to the NPA. U.S. Navy Pacific Fleet Commander Admiral James Lyons appeared to confirm this in May 1987 when he said that the Soviets were supplying aid to the NPA.[67] Both claims were denied by the Soviet Union and by Philippine authorities, despite numerous press reports in Manila of Soviet logistic support, arms supplies, and even training by Soviet (KGB) personnel on the spot.[68] There were also reports of East European arms supplies, particularly from Czechoslovakia, reaching the Philippine Communists through Malaysia. If any of these reports were true, it would have marked a change in the Soviet position from opposition to active support.

Such a change might be suggested by the moderately anti-Aquino nature of Soviet reporting on the Philippines. It could also result from the reported rise of pro-Soviet elements in the Communist NPA and a new openness to Soviet aid on the part of the Philippine Communist Party.[69] One might then speculate that the reported new relationship with Moscow accounted for Soviet bloc material aid and thus, presumably, support for the many terrorist as well as guerrilla actions conducted by the Philippine Communists, as well as by the Moros. By the same token, a new, sympathetic relationship between Moscow and the illegal Philippine Communist Party could also account for the support in the party for initiating such parliamentary (that is, nonviolent) actions as running candidates in local elections. It might also account for the slight reduction in the number of armed actions in 1988. In other words, as in the case of other movements such as the PLO, Soviet assistance enabling armed struggle, including terrorism, might actually be accompanied by restraint and persuasion in accordance with Moscow's preference for political, nonarmed struggle. Yet, before drawing any conclusions, it must be noted that as late as October 1987, there was still strong evidence that the Philippine Communists and the NPA had not actually been successful in gaining any Soviet aid.[70]

There has been another, somewhat clearer case of increased (possibly even new) support for terrorist operations since Gorbachev came to power. In 1986, the Soviet media began to report favorably on incidents in Pakistan conducted by Pathan nationalists, and there were reports of Soviet arms supplies to the Pathans and other groups in Pakistan.[71] In 1987, Pathan and other terrorist actions in Pakistan, inspired and supported by the Soviet puppet regime in Afghanistan, became the most prominent terrorist phenomenon in the world. According to the U.S. State Department, Afghan intelligence operating in Pakistan was responsible for two-thirds of the incidents of international terrorism in 1987.[72] The Pakistani government traced the sharp increase in incidents to Najibullah's rise to power in Kabul and refrained from blaming the Soviets directly.[73] Soviet relations with Najibullah were far from the indirect and limited influence Moscow exercised over parties in Latin America or movements elsewhere in the Third World. It would be difficult, therefore, to believe that such widespread and frequent activity of Afghan agents, officially and undoubtedly effectively subordinate to the KGB, could be conducted without Soviet approval and, probably, assistance.

There were, in fact, two theories about Soviet involvement. The first was that at least some of the incidents had been mounted by Afghan agents without Soviet authorization, in an attempt to sabotage Soviet-Pakistani talks and thus prevent Soviet withdrawal from Afghanistan.[74] The second theory was that the Soviets organized the terrorist campaign to pressure the Pakistani government to halt support for Afghan rebels and the activities of Afghan refugees in Pakistan. According to this version, the Soviets had increased their direct involvement in recruiting and training terrorists in Pakistan as of August 1987 and no longer sought to conceal their role so as to impress upon Pakistan the risks of continued support for the Afghan rebels.[75] The incidents did decline in 1988 as the Soviet withdrawal progressed toward its increasingly certain conclusion.

Both the Philippine and Pakistani cases raise serious questions about who in the Kremlin has been deciding Soviet policy toward terrorism. In the case of the Philippines, for example, there have been reports of a dispute between the International Department of the Central Committee of the Soviet Communist Party and the KGB. Soviet reluctance to become involved, a policy preference of the International Department, might account for both the sporadic and, indeed, uncertain nature of the reported Soviet aid to the NPA and for the encouragement of political methods. At the same time, the KGB's interest in involvement has been said to account for the rumored East European arms supplies.[76] Afghan support of terrorism in Pakistan, similarly, might be explained by the dominance of military decision makers in the period preceding the Soviet decision to withdraw, perhaps in desperate search for military answers to their losing battle in Afghanistan. Given evidence of the military's dissatisfaction with its role under Gorbachev's new approach to armed struggle, it is conceivable that GRU personnel, like KGB operatives, have been given somewhat more freedom of action or possibly even independent orders — different from those emanating from the CPSU — by their superiors in Moscow.

The replacement of KGB chief Viktor Chebrikov in late 1988 may have been designed to ensure stricter observance of new thinking in operations abroad. Chebrikov's replacement, Vladimir Kriuchkov, who was subsequently promoted to full membership in the Politburo in September 1989, had spent most of his career in overseas assignments. There is reason to believe that he was chosen because of his sympathy with Gorbachev's line of thinking. Kriuchkov was closely associated with Gorbachev's mentor, Yuri Andropov, having served under Andropov in the Soviet embassy in Budapest in 1956, during the period of the Hungarian revolution, even before Andropov's appointment as head of the KGB in 1967.

Compartmentalization in the past may have accounted for the distinct differences between official, academic, and journalistic positions, on the one hand, and Soviet behavior in the field, on the other hand.[77] Such differences were indeed apparent with regard to national liberation movements as well as revolutionary groups, which often included groups publicly opposed by Moscow but appearing to receive indirect if not actual direct Soviet help in the form of arms, training, and logistical assistance. It is possible, however, that the apparent ambivalence that was noted with regard to a number of movements — from the IRA to the PLO — insofar as their methods were concerned, is due today less to compartmentalization, and even intentional disinformation, than to actual differences of opinion or competition between the foreign policy institutions in Moscow. There is no hard evidence of such differences; their existence is purely speculative. The possibility of such an explanation of apparent contradictions or ambiguities in Soviet behavior cannot be ruled out, however.

Soviet and Soviet-backed Targets

Obviously, when terrorism, or any armed action, has been used by groups against Soviet-supported regimes — such as the activities of rebels in Afghanistan, the Eritreans and Tigrans in Ethiopia, the rebels in Mozambique, occasionally the Kurds in Iraq, the contras in Nicaragua, or elements attacking Soviet targets — Moscow has been quick to condemn the perpetrators and to demand their punishment as well as sanctions against those who support such groups. The Soviet bloc countries themselves have been frequent victims of airplane hijackings (from 1977 to 1986, there were 38 hijackings in East European countries compared with 34 in Western Europe, according to U.S. figures); for this reason, Aeroflot pilots, for example, carry handguns.[78] There have also been terrorist attacks (mainly the planting of bombs) inside the Soviet Union and East European countries.[79] Soviet participants in the 1989 Soviet-American conference on terrorism revealed that over 60 Soviet civilians, diplomats, and military personnel have been killed in international terrorist attacks outside of war zones since the mid-1980s alone.[80]

Soviet policy under Gorbachev as well as his predecessors has generally been to refuse any negotiations with hijackers. Usually special antiterrorist police units have been employed to bring about a conclusion to such incidents. The December 1988 incident, when a Soviet plane was flown to Israel, was something of an exception. On that occasion the Soviets acquiesced to the hijackers' demand for a plane and permitted them to board with their weapons in exchange for release of a busload of children they had hijacked.

The most spectacular event against a Soviet target occurred in October 1985, early in the Gorbachev era, when four Soviet diplomats were kidnapped in Beirut. In this instance, too, the Soviet Union did not negotiate with the kidnappers, but rather brought pressure to bear on its ally Syria to act as intermediary with the Islamic perpetrators. Graphic accounts reached the West claiming that the Soviets obtained the release of the three surviving hostages by kidnapping a relative of one of the kidnappers, castrating him, and sending his mutilated parts to the captors.[81] A less imaginative account explained that the Soviets engaged in a month of intensive intelligence work and, with the aid of the Syrians, located the whereabouts of the hostages as well as the identity of their captors. The KGB then made personal threats on the captors and their families to obtain the hostages' release.[82] Still another, more reliable account claimed that the kidnappings were perpetrated by a Sunni fundamentalist group under military siege by the Syrians in Tripoli. With Iranian and PLO assistance, the Soviets arranged a Syrian agreement to lift the siege in exchange for release of the hostages.

Whatever the actual facts, this case has been cited as an example of the decisive, if brutal, action the Soviets are willing and capable of taking to obtain the release of their own people, in contrast to the unsuccessful tactics employed by the West.[83] Even Soviet citizens, however, have questioned the dangerous and possibly inhumane policy of refusing to negotiate or in any way comply with terrorists' demands to save victims.[84] Under Gorbachev, however, the Soviets have been more willing to cooperate with Western counterterrorist officials, to provide information on Soviet methods, and reportedly to share some relevant intelligence.

Conclusion

Before Gorbachev assumed power, the Soviet Union viewed terrorism as one of several forms of armed struggle used by liberation or revolutionary groups. Armed struggle itself, although assisted and often supported, was considered less preferable to political action because of the dangers involved in armed conflict. Terrorism was the least preferred form of armed struggle, for a number of practical, political, and even ideological reasons. Hesitation about armed struggle and opposition to the use of terrorism did not, however, impede Soviet willingness to arm, train, and otherwise assist actions by groups that Moscow wanted to support for local, regional, or global reasons. Nevertheless, Soviet preferences were conveyed to their clients, and the training (and often the arms supplied) reflected the priority Moscow gave to conventional warfare and sabotage over guerrilla warfare and terrorism.

Some changes did occur as a result of the new thinking introduced into Soviet foreign policy by Gorbachev. The interest in eliminating regional conflicts and crisis situations has led to the exclusive pursuit of political solutions, rather than a mere preference for peaceful means over armed struggle. If Soviet support for armed struggle is to be phased out, it goes without saying that terrorism, the least preferred form of armed struggle, should also be abandoned. Gorbachev has made all these connections, directly placing terror in the context of regional conflict as one of the consequences of such conflicts, and he has called for political means both as a solution to conflict and an alternative to the use of terrorism. These doctrinal changes can be traced mainly to mid-1987, although they were outlined as early as Gorbachev's speech to the CPSU Congress in 1986.

There have been two concrete results, also traceable to roughly mid-1987, of this doctrinal or policy change. First, the new policy has resulted in the Soviets' advising and possibly pressuring at least some groups, such as the PLO and the ANC, to seek political settlements and curb armed actions, particularly the use of such extreme measures as terrorism. This has been reflected more in discussions about and with the movements, including, in some cases, a description of their acts as "terrorism," than in an actual reduction in the supply of arms or training. Evidence of the latter is very difficult to obtain, and available information provides no clues as to whether instructions to KGB and GRU personnel in the field have actually been changed. There is even some evidence of increased or new Soviet involvement with groups conducting terrorism, possibly in the Philippines or Pakistan. How much of this can be attributed to the independent action of local Communists, as is probably the case with terrorist actions by Lebanese Communists, rather than to orders from Moscow or even from local Soviet operatives? Although this question is difficult to answer, there has been a decline since 1987 in terrorist action by most of the groups believed to be supported by the Soviet Union.

Second, the new policy has resulted in official Soviet attention to the issue of terrorism and a declared willingness to cooperate in eliminating it. The Soviet regime has thus advocated joint international steps—in keeping with Gorbachev's view of an "interdependent" world—to deal with the issue. This has been reflected in Soviet proposals for an international conference on counterterrorism, the actual organization of an unofficial conference on the subject in Moscow in early 1989, and Soviet participation, or pursuit of participation, in such meetings in the West. There have also been reports that the Soviets have cooperated with and shared intelligence with Western countries on Libyan or Palestinian operatives, for example, particularly in Eastern Europe. Although the Soviets have not ceased their customary criticism and accusations of both U.S. support for state terrorism and provocative measures by the Israeli Mossad, their accusations have been greatly reduced in both volume and acidity. Indeed, following the speedy Israeli return of a hijacked Soviet plane and the hijackers, Moscow radio conveyed KGB willingness to cooperate with the Mossad and the CIA.

On the whole, Gorbachev's new thinking does contain a new attitude toward terrorism. It was summed up in Shevardnadze's comments to the UN General Assembly on September 26, 1989:

> Violence on national, ethnic or religious grounds must no longer be tolerated. . . . No support or sympathy should be extended to the so-called movements that allow actions humiliating other nations, or use terrorist, barbaric and inhuman methods in waging their struggle.

There are even signs that some steps toward implementation of this view are taking place. Yet, like so many other components of perestroika, the enunciated policy and proposed changes are still far from completion and full application. This much is sure – the direction has changed. Only the future can reveal the extent to which the proclaimed goals can or will be achieved.

Notes

The Library of Congress system of transliteration has been used except where a different transliteration appears in the source.

Chapter 1

1. V. I. Lenin, "Left-Wing Communism, an Infantile Disorder," *Collected Works*, vol. 31 (Moscow: Progress Publishers, 1966), 17–117. See also Ze'ev Avyansky, *Personal Terror (Hateror ha ishi)* (Tel Aviv: Kibbutz Hameuchad, 1977); William Pomeroy, ed., *Guerrilla Warfare and Marxism* (London: Lawrence and Wishart, 1969), 75–121; Robert Freedman, "Soviet Policy towards International Terrorism," in Yonah Alexander, ed., *International Terrorism: National, Regional and Global Perspectives* (New York: Praeger, 1976), 115–116.

2. Quoted in the Ministry of Defense–Africa Institute study: V. L. Tiagunenko et al., *Vooruzhennaia bor'ba narodov Afriki za svobodu i nezavisimost'* (Moscow: Ministerstvo Oborony-SSSR, Nauka, 1974), 44–45.

3. See, for example, Lenin, *Collected Works*, 189.

4. See Daniel Papp, "National Liberation during Detente: The Soviet Outlook," *International Journal* 32 (1976–1977): 82–99; Pomeroy, *Guerrilla Warfare*; Feliks Gross, *Violence in Politics* (The Hague: Mouton, 1972); William Griffith, *The Sino-Soviet Rift* (Cambridge, Mass.: MIT Press, 1964), 241–288.

5. *Sovetskaia voennaia entsiklopediia* (Moscow: Voenizdat, 1980), 30; Marshal Nikolai Ogarkov, ed., *Voyenni entsiklopedicheskii slovar'* (Moscow: Voenizdat, 1983), 736.

6. For this and the following discussion of the theoretical formulations regarding terrorism during the Brezhnev era, see Galia Golan, *The Soviet Union and National Liberation Movements in the Third World* (London: Unwin and Hyman, 1988), chap. 4.

7. A. I. Sobolev, "Leninskaia kontseptsiia mnogoobraziia putei sotsial'nogo razvitiia," *Voprosy istorii KPSS* no. 4 (1980): 41–52.

8. S. L. Agaev, "Levyi radikalizm, revoliutsionnyi demokratizm i nauchyni sotsializm v stranakh Vostoka," *Rabochii klass i sovremennyi mir* no. 3 (1984): 134–135; see also, Joan Barth Urban, "Contemporary Soviet Perspectives on Revolution in the West," *Orbis* 28, no. 4 (1976): 1371; Jerry Hough, "The Evolving Soviet Debate on Latin America," *Latin American Research Review* 16, no. 1 (1981): 131–132; Edme Dominguez Reyes, "Soviet Academic Views on the Caribbean and Central America," Paper presented at the International Association of Slavic Studies Conference, Washington, D. C., 1985, pp. 5–6.

9. Tiagunenko et al., *Vooruzhennaia bor'ba*, 55.

10. Ibid.

11. Col. V. Andrianov, "Partizanskaia voina i voennaia strategiia," *Voenno-istoricheskii zhurnal* no. 7 (1975): 29–31.

12. See Hough, "Evolving Soviet Debate," 131–132; Reyes, "Soviet Academic Views," 5–6.

13. Viktor Vitiuk, *Leftist Terrorism* (Moscow: Progress Publishers, 1984), 23, 24.

14. Tiagunenko et al., *Vooruzhennaia bor'ba*, 301.

15. Ibid., 361.

16. Pomeroy, *Guerrilla Warfare*, 75–121; Gross, *Violence in Politics*, 32; Alexander, ed., *International Terrorism*, 115–116; Nathan Leites, *A Study of Bolshevism* (Glencoe, Ill.: Free Press, 1953), 341; Stefan Possony, *A Century of Conflict* (Chicago: Regenoy, 1953), 224–225.

17. Col. Evgenii Dolgopolov, "Razoblachenie burzhuaznykh i maoistkikh fal'sifikatorov istorii lokal'nykh voin," *Voenno-istoricheskii zhurnal* no. 6 (1980): 61–62.

18. Sobolev, 49–50.

19. Vitiuk, *Leftist Terrorism*, 26.

20. Antonio Jannazzo, in "Revolution and Democracy: International Scientific Conference," *World Marxist Review* 22, no. 10 (1979): 38.

21. Tommy O'Flaherty in ibid., 39.

22. Vladimir Fedorov, "Levyi ekstremizm v politicheskoi zhizni stran Vostoka," *Aziia i Afrika segodnia* no. 5 (1983): 13–16.

23. A. Kartzev, "Terrorizm orudie imperializma i reaktsii," *Kommunist vooruzhennykh sil* no. 23 (December 1983): 79.

24. See, for example, *Pravda*, January 7, 1973 and December 19, 1973; TASS, November 27, 1972 and May 20, 1974.

25. Vladimir Terekhov, "International Terrorism and the Fight against It," *New Times* no. 11 (1974): 20–21.

26. *New York Times*, September 27, 1972.

27. *Izvestiia*, July 30, 1974.

28. See Galia Golan, *The Soviet Union and the Palestine Liberation Organization: An Uneasy Alliance* (New York: Praeger, 1980), 219–227, for Soviet responses to specific Palestinian acts of terrorism.

29. Freedman, "Soviet Policy towards International Terrorism," 115–147.

30. *Pravda*, February 21, 1981.

31. Ibid., March 4, 1973.

32. Dolgopolov, *Razoblachenie*, 61–62.

33. V. Iordanski, "The Policy of Neo-colonialism in Action," *International Affairs* no. 6 (1981): 84. See also V. Efremov, "Mezhdunarodnyi terrorizm-orudie imperializma i reaktsii," *Aziia i Afrika segodnia* no. 7 (1981): 24–26; *Izvestiia*, October 15, 1981 (Anatoli Gromyko), February 8, 1981, and June 17, 1981; *Pravda*, February 1, 1981 and October 19, 1981.

34. TASS, September 22, 1981.

35. *Pravda*, February 23, 1981.

36. TASS, March 20, 1981.

Chapter 2

1. See, for example, Claire Sterling, *The Terror Network* (New York: Berkley Books, 1981); Roberta Goren, *The Soviet Union and Terrorism* (London: Allen and Unwin, 1984); Uri Ra'anan, Robert Pfaltzgraff, Richard Shultz, Ernst Halperin, Igor Lukes, *Hydra of Carnage* (Lexington, Ma.: Lexington Books, 1986); Ray

Cline and Yonah Alexander, *Terrorism: The Soviet Connection* (New York: Crane Russak, 1984).

2. *International Herald Tribune*, April 28, 1987; Wilhelm Dietl, "Eastern Europe: The Quiet Business," in Aaron Karp, ed., "Shades of Grey: The Hidden Arms Trade Today," Stockholm International Peace Research Institute, 1987, unpublished.

3. Shlomi Elad and Ariel Merari, *The Soviet Bloc and World Terrorism* (Tel Aviv: Jaffee Center for Strategic Studies, 1984), 22–26.

4. Ibid., 21–25.

5. See, for example, article in the *Washington Times*, May 14, 1986, citing the International Institute of Strategic Studies; see Elad and Merari, *The Soviet Bloc*, 22–24, on indirect supplies.

6. Elad and Merari, *The Soviet Bloc*, 21–25; Walter Laqueur, *The Age of Terrorism* (Boston: Little, Brown and Co., 1987), 274–275.

7. Elad and Merari, *The Soviet Bloc*, 12–13.

8. Golan, *Soviet Union and National Liberation Movements*, 261–363.

9. Laqueur, *Age of Terrorism*, 272.

10. V. Pavlov, "The Death of Prisoner No. 1066," *New Times* no. 20 (May 1981): 21 (quoting Michael O'Riordan, general secretary of the Communist Party of Ireland).

11. Ibid.; V. Zhitomirsky, "N. Ireland Tension," *New Times* no. 18 (May 1981): 15; I. Titov, "Northern Ireland: Ten Years of Repression," *New Times* no. 51 (December 1982): 22; V. Zhitomirsky, "Cold-Blooded Murder," *New Times* no. 36 (1981): 10.

12. Andrei Nikitin (reader's letter), "Thinking of Northern Ireland," *New Times* no. 30 (July 1981): 15.

13. Tiagunenko et al., *Vooruzhennaia bor'ba*, 361.

14. "The Way of the Anti-Imperialist Struggle in Tropical Africa," *World Marxist Review* no. 8 (1971): 31; A. M. Khazanov, "Angola: bor'ba za nezavisimost'," *Voprosy istorii* no. 8 (1978): 118–119.

15. David Martin and Phyllis Johnson, *The Struggle for Zimbabwe* (London: Faber and Faber, 1981), 146; *Le Monde Diplomatique*, May 1970, p. 11; John Day, "The Insignificance of Tribe in the African Politics of Zimbabwe-Rhodesia," *Journal of Commonwealth and Comparative Politics* 8, no. 1 (1980): 89–93; Thomas Gerald-Scheepers, "African Resistance in Rhodesia," *African Perspectives* no. 1 (1976): 125–126.

16. *New African*, November 1978, p. 81 and May 1979, p. 34; *Africa* no. 75 (1977): 25.

17. Evgeny Tarabrin, "Peking's Maneuvres in Africa," *New Times* no. 22 (1972): 19; Tiagunenko et al., *Vooruzhennaia bor'ba*, 73.

18. Tom Lodge, "The African National Congress in South Africa, 1967–1983: Guerrilla War and Armed Propaganda," *Journal of Contemporary African Studies* 3, no. 1/2 (1983–1984): 160.

19. Martin and Johnson, *Struggle for Zimbabwe*, 10.

20. *To The Point* 7, no. 31 (1978): 13; Christopher Coker, "Decolonization in the Seventies: Rhodesia and the Dialectic of National Liberation," *Round Table* no. 274 (1979): 122–136; *Africa Confidential* 19, no. 21 (1978): 1.

21. *Pravda*, May 23, 1977.

22. *Daily Telegraph*, May 28, 1978.

23. Anatoly Gromyko, "Neo-colonialism's Maneuvres in Southern Africa," *International Affairs* no. 12 (1977): 98–99.

24. See, for example, *Izvestiia*, January 26, 1978; *Pravda*, March 28, 1978. See also, *Pravda*, September 23, 1979; Moscow radio in English, May 15 and 21, 1979 and December 6, 1979.

25. *Africa Research Bulletin*, February 1–28, 1978; *Financial Times*, February 4, 1978; *Africa Confidential* 20, no. 9: 2; Tiagunenko et al., *Vooruzhennaia bor'ba*, 300; "Iug Afriki: revoliutsionnyi protsess neobratim," *Aziia i Afrika segodnia* no. 9 (1979): 29.

26. *Pravda*, October 24, 1976; *Krasnaia zvezda*, May 25, 1977; P. I. Manchkha, *Aktual'nye problemy sovremennoi Afriki* (Moscow: Politizdat, 1979), 264; TASS, August 11, 1976; "Iug Afriki," 23–24; N. D. Turkatenko, "Raschety i proschety Vashingtona v Iuzhoi Afrike," *SShA: ekonomika, politika, ideologiia* no. 2 (1977): 33.

27. *Pravda*, October 10, 1983; Andrei Urnov, "The Windhoek Farce," *New Times*, no. 29 (1985): 22; A. Kiva, "The Struggle against the Remnants of Colonialism and Neocolonialism," *International Affairs* no. 3 (1981): 51–52; V. Shubin, "Fictions and Realities," *New Times* no. 50 (1985): 13; Iu. Gorbunov, "Militarizatsiia obrechennogo rezhima," *Aziia i Afrika segodnia* no. 8 (1982): 29; *Pravda*, July 31, 1984; TASS, August 11, 1976; K. Vitaliev, "Imperialist Policy and the Conflict in South Africa," *International Affairs* no. 11 (1982): 46.

28. *Africa Contemporary Record, 1978–1979*, pp. A-19–20;

Africa Confidential 19, no. 13 (1978): 1, and *Africa Confidential* 20, no. 8 (1979): 1.

29. T. Bonga et al., "Statement on the Expulsion from the ANC(SA)," Hoover Archives, London, December 27, 1975, p. 12.

30. "Dvizhenie soprotivleniia rasistam usilivaetsia," *Mezhdunarodnaia zhizn'* no. 4 (1985): 131 (Nzo interview); V. Shubin, "Mezhdu nakoval'nei i molotom," *Mezhdunarodnaia zhizn'* no. 3 (1985): 36–37.

31. V. Shubin, "What the Camera Is Not Focussed On," *New Times* no. 31 (1985): 10–11.

32. *AfricAsia* no. 33 (1986): 15–16. Slovo called for "mass political struggle coupled with an intensification of revolutionary violence" in *The Guardian*, August 17, 1986.

33. Aryeh Yodfat, "The USSR and the Palestinians," *New Outlook* no. 19 (1976): 31.

34. Elad and Merari, *The Soviet Bloc*, 29–32.

Chapter 3

1. Marshal S. Akhromeyev, *Voyenni entsiklopedicheskii slovar'* (Moscow: Voenizdat, 1986), 737.

2. *Pravda*, February 26, 1986.

3. D. Volskii, *Izvestiia*, December 24, 1987.

4. Vladimir Petrovskii, "A New Concept of World Politics," *New Times* no. 14 (April 1988): 5. (Emphasis added.)

5. A. Kiva, "Great October and the National-Liberation Movement," *Aziia i Afrika segodnia* no. 11 (November 1987): 6.

6. "Latin America: Democracy Must Be Won, Not Waited For," *World Marxist Review* no. 7 (July 1988): 99.

7. Evgenii Primakov, "Sovetskaia politika v regionalnikh konfliktakh," *Mezhdunarodnaia zhizn'* no. 5 (May 1988): 3–9.

8. "The USSR and the Third World," *International Affairs* no. 12 (1988): 137.

9. Richard Ovinnikov, "Glavnye slagaemye ustoichivogo mira," *Mezhdunarodnaia zhizn'* no. 5 (May 1988): 16.

10. "Perestroika, the 19th Party Conference and Foreign Policy," *International Affairs* no. 7 (July 1988): 14. (Emphasis added.)

11. Andrei Kozyrev, "Confidence and the Balance of Interests," *Mezhdunarodnaia zhizn'* no. 10 (October 1988): 3–12; En-

glish quotations are from *International Affairs* no. 11 (November 1988): 8, 10, 11.

12. Anatoly Dobrynin, "Soviet Foreign Policy: Basic Principles and New Thinking," *World Marxist Review* no. 3 (March 1988): 22–23.

13. This was the wording of the conference resolution: "[The conference] confirms that only a political approach toward resolving the contradictions of world development and regulating conflict situations opens up the opportunity for the USSR to play its historically predestined role in ensuring the survival and further progress of mankind." *Pravda*, July 5, 1988.

14. Eduard Shevardnadze, "The 19th All-Union CPSU Conference: Foreign Policy and Diplomacy," *International Affairs* no. 10 (October 1988): 12–19.

15. *Stability and Security—A Common Concern* (Moscow: Novosti, 1986), 64.

16. See, for example, Gorbachev's speech honoring Prime Minister Thatcher, *Pravda*, April 1, 1987 or honoring UN Secretary General Perez de Cuellar, *Pravda*, January 10, 1987.

17. Col. Gen. Vladimir Lobov, "The Armed Forces and New Thinking," *New Times* no. 8 (March 1988): 12; Marshal S. F. Akhromeyev, "The Doctrine of Preventing War, Defending Peace and Socialism," *World Marxist Review* no. 12 (December 1987): 26.

18. Col. Gen. Dmitry Volkogonov, "The Anti-War Doctrine," *New Times* no. 25 (June 1987): 14–15. This was a reversal of positions he expressed as late as January 1987, as mentioned later.

19. Col. B. Lytov, "70th Anniversary of USSR Armed Forces," *Aviatsiya i kosmonavtika* no. 10 (October 1987): 39–41, in JPRS-UAC-88-004, April 28, 1988, p. 24; *Krasnaia zvezda*, September 25, 1987.

20. Raymond Garthoff, "New Thinking in Soviet Military Doctrine," *The Washington Quarterly* 2, no. 3 (Summer 1988): 134–137.

21. *Pravda*, July 27, 1987. A year later a Soviet discussion of differences of opinion on the new military doctrine placed Yazov in the category of those who did not agree to the abandonment of offense in favor of a purely defensive doctrine. *APN Military Bulletin* (Moscow) no. 10 (May 1988): 5–8. The discussion is beyond the scope of this paper, however.

22. General D. T. Yazov, *Na strazhe sotsializma i mira* (Moscow: Voenizdat, 1987), 31.

23. *Krasnaia zvezda*, June 25, 1988.

24. A steady decline in the number of such articles is clearly detectable from 1985–1986 to late 1987 and 1988 as, presumably, the new thinking became more entrenched.

25. Col. Gen. N. Chervov, "Moguchii faktor mira," *Mezhdunarodnaia zhizn'* no. 2 (February 1988): 11.

26. Lt. Gen. of Aviation V. Serebryannikov, "Sootnoshenie politicheskikh i voennykh sredstv v zashchite sotsializma," *Kommunist vooruzhennykh sil* no. 18 (September 1987): 13.

27. *Krasnaia zvezda*, January 3, 1988 and June 7, 1988.

28. Nikolai Efimov, "Revoliutsionnyi protsess i sovremennost," *Kommunist vooruzhennykh sil* no. 7 (April 1987): 86–88.

29. Lt. Gen. D. Volkogonov in answer to question on "The 27th CPSU Congress on War and the Armed Forces," *Argumenty i Fakty*, April 15, 1986 in JPRS-UMA-86-040, July 22, 1986, p. 15; Lt. Gen. D. Volkogonov, "Chelovecheskii faktor: puti adtivizatsii," *Kommunist vooruzhennykh sil* no. 2 (January 1987): 15.

30. Yevgeny Dolgopolov, "Working for Independence: National Liberation Wars in a Nuclear Age," *Soviet Military Review* no. 7 (1987): 50–51.

31. *Krasnaia zvezda*, April 30, 1988.

32. Col. Vasily Login, "The Revolution Must Defend Itself," *Soviet Military Review* no. 4 (April 1988): 13.

33. Col. Timofei Uzhegov (ret.) and Maj. Sergei Menyailo, "Partisan Warfare," *Soviet Military Review* no. 5 (May 1988): 42–44, 39.

Chapter 4

1. Efimov, "Revoliutsionnyi protsess," 86. In an earlier article Efimov said that national liberation struggles and those against dictatorships "have nothing in common with terrorism." Thus he defended the "guerrillas of El Salvador, the patriots of Namibia and South Africa, and the fighters of the Palestine resistance movement. . . ." Major Nikolai Yefimov, "The Calculations and Miscalculations of the 'New Crusaders,'" *Soviet Military Review* no. 8 (August 1986): 51.

2. Dolgopolov, "Working for Independence," 50.

3. *Izvestiia*, May 31, 1986.

4. For example, Artyom Sergiyev, "The Present Stage of the Non-Aligned Movement," *International Affairs* no. 12 (December 1986): 109, quoting the Harare conference of nonaligned states.

5. *Izvestiia*, June 20, 1988, responding to a broadcast reference made to a "Palestinian terrorist" by a political satirist during a Moscow beauty competition; *al-Anba* (Kuwait), May 27, 1988, telephone interview with Novosti Middle East specialist Aleksandr Smirnov.

6. *Pravda*, September 17, 1986.

7. Ibid., October 6, 1986.

8. For example, L. Koryavin in *Izvestiia*, January 29, 1986.

9. *Izvestiia*, September 25, 1986; *Pravda*, September 26, 1986.

10. Gorbachev speech in India, November 27, 1986; *Stability and Security*, 39–40.

11. *Selskaia zhizn'*, September 27, 1986; TASS, January 8, 1986 and April 11, 1986; *Izvestiia*, January 29, 1986 and May 31, 1986; *Pravda*, October 6, 1986. The May 31, 1986 *Izvestiia* round table was entitled "Terrorism – An Instrument of Neo-Globalism"; a number of books took this title or similar ones such as "Terrorism and Imperialism."

12. *Izvestiia*, March 9, 1986; *Pravda*, March 10, 1986.

13. TASS, December 18, 1985 and January 8, 1986; *Izvestiia*, January 29, 1986; *Selskaia zhizn'*, September 27, 1986.

14. Moscow radio, December 4, 1985; Igor Beliaev in *Literaturnaia gazeta*, January 29, 1986 and June 18, 1986; Evgeny Korshunov, "Who the Terrorists Are," *New Times* no. 14 (April 1986): 11–12; *Izvestiia*, May 8, 1986; Maj. Gen. L. Nikitin and Col. O. Ivanov, "Imperialism's Intrigues in the Near East," *Zarubezhnoye voyennoye obozreniye* no. 6 (June 1987): 10–16, in *JPRS-UFM-87-008*, December 29, 1987, p. 9.

15. TASS, August 23, 1988; Moscow domestic service, August 24, 1988 (in FBIS-SOV-88-164, August 24, 1988, p. 8 and FBIS-SOV-88-165, August 25, 1988, p. 4).

16. *Pravda*, January 5, 1987 and April 5, 1987; *Izvestiia*, January 9 and 27, 1987, May 10, 1987, and June 11, 1987; *Pravda*, January 17, 1988 (Gorbachev); M. D. Nesuk, *Pro terrorizm* (L'viv: Kaminiar, 1986).

17. For example, Igor Beliaev in *Literaturnaia gazeta*, January 29 and June 18, 1986.

18. See, for example, N. B. Krylov and Iuri A. Reshetov, "Gosudarstvennyi terrorizm—ugroza mezhdunarodnoi bezopasnosti," *Sovetsko gosudarstvo i pravo* no. 2 (1987): 78–84.

19. Andrei Grachev, "The Boomerang of Terrorism," *New Times* no. 42 (October 1987).

20. *Pravda*, September 7, 1986; *Izvestiia*, September 8, 1986. See also, Demchenko in *Pravda*, September 9, 1986 or Yuri Romantsov in *Selskaia zhizn'*, September 27, 1986. (Emphasis added.)

21. *Pravda*, October 17, 1986.

22. TASS, October 31, 1988.

23. *Soviet Military Review*, March 1988, p. 55.

24. *Izvestiia*, January 28, 1987, February 11, 1987, July 25, 1987, August 2, 1987, and May 17, 1988.

25. See, for example, *Izvestiia*, August 30, 1987, September 2, 1987, and October 4, 1987.

26. *Sovetskaia rossiya*, June 18, 1988.

27. *Izvestiia*, July 25, 1987; TASS, April 11, 12, and 19, 1988.

28. TASS, April 19, 1988.

29. *New York Times*, December 7, 1985.

30. *The Economist*, December 14, 1985, p. 39; *New York Times*, December 18, 1985.

31. *New York Times*, October 10, 1985.

32. *Pravda*, February 26, 1986.

33. *The* (London) *Times*, December 8, 1985.

34. Mikhail Gorbachev, *Perestroika: New Thinking for Our Country and the World* (London: Collins, 1987), 173.

35. *Izvestiia*, May 31, 1986.

36. TASS, September 10, 1986.

37. Deutsche Presse Agent (DPA), April 23, 1986; *Ha'aretz*, June 20, 1986.

38. *Washington Post*, May 17, 1986.

39. *New York Times*, November 20, 1986. For U.S. accusations regarding the March 1986 warnings, see *Washington Post*, April 17, 1986.

40. *Wall Street Journal*, June 19, 1987.

41. Agence France Presse Wire Service (AFP), November 4, 1986.

42. *Washington Post*, March 5, 1989.

43. TASS, February 27, 1987.

44. *New York Times*, April 1, 1987.

45. TASS, July 30, 1987.

46. *Executive Intelligence Review*, June 12, 1987, from Jaffee Center Data Bank.

47. TASS, February 9, 1988; *Pravda*, February 27, 1988. In a *Komsomolskaia Pravda*, September 10, 1986 interview, the 1963 Tokyo Convention (in force since 1969) had been described as inadequate, although Soviet adherence to the subsequent Hague and Montreal Conventions was praised.

48. *Literaturnaia gazeta*, March 15, 1989.

49. This and the following information on the Moscow conference are based on the following: accounts of participants Brian Jenkins, John Marks, Robin Wright, and Michael Stohl in the *Washington Post*, March 5, 1989, and in the *Los Angeles Times*, January 27 and 28, 1989; interviews with some of the Soviet participants; and *Literaturnaia gazeta*, March 15, 1989.

50. Ibid.

51. Ibid.

52. Also missing were those who have written on terrorism in the past, such as Grachev, Vitiuk, and Fedorov.

53. *Literaturnaia gazeta*, March 15, 1989.

Chapter 5

1. "The 'Breakthrough': A Joint Effort," *New Times* no. 19 (May 1988): 13.

2. "The USSR and the Third World," 137–143.

3. Galina Sidorova, "Diplomacy and Glasnost," *New Times* no. 12 (March 1988): 20.

4. *Literaturnaia gazeta*, March 15, 1989.

5. Konstantin Geivandov, *Izvestiia*, March 30, 1988.

6. A. Ignatenko in *Pravda*, November 16, 1987.

7. *Al-Anba*, May 27, 1988; *Izvestiia*, August 6, 1987.

8. TASS, November 1, 1988.

9. Dimtry Zgersky, "Yasser Arafat in Moscow," *New Times* no. 16 (April 1988): 9.

10. Leonid Medvedko, "A Time to Throw Stones and a Time to Collect Them," *New Times* no. 36 (September 1988): 16.

11. *Sovetskaia Rossiya*, October 26, 1988.

12. TASS, April 10, 1988. (Emphasis added.)

13. See commentary by Aleksandr Bovin in *Izvestiia*, January 6, 1989.

14. *Izvestiia*, January 11, 1989; *Pravda*, January 1, 1989.

15. Ariel Merari and Anat Kurz, *INTER: International Terrorism in 1987* (Jerusalem: Jaffee Center for Strategic Studies, 1988), 17–32.

16. Ibid., 78.

17. Ibid., 27.

18. *New York Times*, January 26, 1988; *Wall Street Journal*, June 19, 1987; Merari and Kurz, *INTER*, 29.

19. Vladimir Nosenko, "Sowing Fear Is Not a Way of Building Peace," *New Times* no. 12 (March 21–27, 1989): 9–11.

20. *Pravda*, May 29, 1986.

21. *Literaturnaia gazeta*, January 18, 1989.

22. TASS, September 17, 1986. The same day *Pravda* also published a condemnation of the French Communist Party, denying Western accusations that Moscow aided international terrorists or that Marxists were behind these acts.

23. *Pravda*, May 29, 1986; *Izvestiia*, June 9, 1987 (visit of Supreme Soviet delegation to Libya).

24. Merari and Kurz, *INTER*, 14; *New York Times*, April 1, 1987 and August 23, 1988.

25. *Izvestiia*, April 27, 1987.

26. *Pravda*, June 25, 1987 (PLO delegation led by Political Department head Faruk Kaddumi); TASS, February 20, 1989.

27. *Literaturnaia gazeta*, December 7, 1988 (commenting on Israel's speedy extradition of the Soviet hijackers).

28. TASS, February 20, 1989.

29. *Jerusalem Post*, November 9, 1988.

30. *Pravda*, January 4, 5, and 16, 1987.

31. Ibid., January 31, 1987 and May 19, 1987; *Izvestiia*, May 20, 1987.

32. For example, *Izvestiia*, April 18, 1988. The Islamic Jihad appears as a separate organization, but it is controlled by Hizballah. Merari and Kurz, *INTER*, 138.

33. *Newsweek*, November 14, 1983 and *FPI News Service*, October 26, 1984 from Jaffee Center Data Bank.

34. For two excellent analyses of the change in the Soviet attitude toward South Africa, see Philip Nel, "The Current Soviet Approach to South Africa and Its Implications," prepared for the Berkeley-Stanford Project on Soviet International Behavior

(1988); Winrich Kuhne, "A New Realism in Soviet-South African Relations?" *Stiftung Wissenschaft und Politik*, July 1988.

35. Oliver Tambo, "Rumbling Volcano," *New Times* no. 38 (1985): 26 (quoting Johnny Makatini); Temba Hlanganani, "The Greatest Moment of My Life," *African Communist* no. 103 (1985): 22–29; V. Rasnitzyn, "The Apartheid Regime under Siege," *International Affairs* no. 10 (1985): 118–120; B. Asoyan, "The Apartheid System Is Doomed," *International Affairs* no. 11 (1985): 53–59.

36. Aaron Shihep, "The Namibian Knot: A Bleeding Wound," *World Marxist Review* no. 4 (April 1988): 122–123.

37. Participants in Leverkusen, West Germany meeting between Soviet Africanists and South African scholars, October 24–27, 1988. See also Kuhne, "A New Realism," 4–6, 10–16.

38. *Pravda*, February 26, 1986.

39. TASS, March 31, 1986; *Pravda*, April 1, 1987; *Izvestiia*, August 5, 1987.

40. For example, B. Asoyan, "Prisoner No. 220/82," *New Times* no. 51 (December 1987): 12–13.

41. Nel, "Current Soviet Approach," 28.

42. Boris Asoyan, "Time to Gather Stones Together," *International Affairs* no. 9 (September 1988): 72. It is interesting to note that this is the same title as the above-mentioned article that was critical of Palestinian extremists.

43. Mzala, "The Volcano of the People's Wrath," *World Marxist Review* no. 7 (July 1988): 121–127.

44. V. Tetiokin, "Real'nosti protivoborstva," *Aziia i Afrika segodnia* no. 11 (1987): 26–28; TASS, October 12, 1988.

45. Philip R. Nel, "The Earnestness of Being Unimportant: The Soviet Union and South Africa," *Soviet Review* 4, no. 6 (November–December 1988): 9.

46. Ibid., 15, 28.

47. Jaffee Center Data Bank, *Risk International*, July 1987.

48. Mikhail Khrobostov, "The Hard Road to a Settlement," *New Times* no. 33 (August 1988): 8–9.

49. Interview with A. L. Adamishin, "Peace Be with You, Africa!" *New Times* no. 21 (May 1988): 18–19.

50. Dmitry Zgersky, "The 'Saharan Wall' the UN Wants to Pull Down," and Boris Bolotin, "Western Sahara – A Problem of Concern to the World Community," *New Times* no. 39 (September 1988): 9–12; *Pravda*, September 29, 1988.

51. *Soviet Review* 4, no. 6 (November–December 1988): 32.

52. Jaffee Center Data Bank, *Risk International*, July 1987.

53. *Ha'aretz*, November 10, 1986.

54. *Izvestiia*, May 17, 1988.

55. See, for example, Yuri Vinogradov, "Conflict in Sri Lanka," *International Affairs* no. 4 (April 1988): 68–73. It is not clear if the PLO has halted its aid to the Tamils, such as the training of Tamils in PFLP (Habash) camps in Syria. Regarding other terrorist activity, see Rodney Tasker, "Trouble from the South," *Far Eastern Economic Review*, May 21, 1987, pp. 46–47.

56. TASS, November 9, 1988.

57. Vladimir Zhitomirsky, "People and Bullets," *New Times* no. 32 (August 1988): 17 and no. 16 (April 1988): 13–16.

58. Yuri Kudimov, "ARENA Bids for Power," *New Times* no. 44 (October 1988): 18–19.

59. Ilya Prizel, "Latin America: The Long March," *National Interest* no. 12 (Summer 1988): 119.

60. Jaffee Center Data Bank, *Risk International*, January 31, 1986.

61. This quotation and the information on the Chilean Communist Party Congress are based on Shirley Christian's account in the *New York Times*, March 12, 1989.

62. Jaffee Center Data Bank, *Counterterrorism*, October 19, 1987.

63. Jaffee Center Data Bank, *Risk International*, May 1983.

64. *Jerusalem Post*, October 30, 1984, citing Australian Prime Minister Robert Hawke. See *Far Eastern Economic Review*, January 16, 1986, pp. 26–27, 40; February 13, 1986, p. 11; May 21, 1987, p. 22; May 28, 1987, pp. 8–9; June 25, 1987, p. 11; July 2, 1987, pp. 30–31; September 3, 1987, pp. 28–29; November 24, 1988, p. 13.

65. *Far Eastern Economic Review*, May 28, 1987, p. 8.

66. Ibid., December 17, 1987, pp. 22–24.

67. Jaffee Center Data Bank, *Risk International*, March 1987; *Defense and Foreign Affairs Weekly*, May 17, 1987.

68. *Defense and Foreign Affairs Weekly*, April 19, 1987; for Philippine government comment, see Gareth Porter, "Philippine Communism after Marcos," *Problems of Communism* 36 (September–October 1987): 17.

69. Porter, "Philippine Communism," 17; *International Herald Tribune*, August 8, 1988; Paul Wolfowitz, "Southeast Asia:

Deferring Hard Choices," *National Interest* no. 12 (Summer 1988): 128–129.

70. Porter, "Philippine Communism," 17.

71. *Far Eastern Economic Review*, March 20, 1986, pp. 50–51. See also "Increased Soviet Pressure on Pakistan," *International Defense Review* no. 5 (1986): 556.

72. *New York Times*, August 23, 1988. Merari and Kurz, *INTER*, 14, lists Iranian-sponsored incidents before Afghanistan, but also notes the significant increase in Afghan activity in Pakistan.

73. *Far Eastern Economic Review*, July 30, 1987, p. 28.

74. Ibid., 7.

75. Ibid., October 29, 1987, pp. 44–45.

76. Wolfowitz, "Southeast Asia: Deferring Hard Choices," 129.

77. Laqueur, *Age of Terrorism*, 277, raises this possibility.

78. Merari and Kurz, *INTER*, 83; *Flight International*, September 12, 1987, p. 6.

79. See, for example, *Sovetskaia Rossiya*, April 23, 1988, on a bomb planted at a Leningrad soccer game; *Pravda*, October 8, 1987 on an explosive device in a Bulgarian train; or *Pravda*, July 12, 1987 on a terrorist attack on a Bulgarian tourist facility.

80. *Los Angeles Times*, January 27, 1989.

81. Ibid., January 16, 1986.

82. *Boston Globe*, March 1, 1987.

83. *Los Angeles Times*, January 16, 1986.

84. *Sovetskaia Rossiya*, April 24, 1988.

Bibliography

Adamishin, Anatoly. "Peace Be with You, Africa." *New Times* no. 21 (1988):18–19.

Agaev, S. L. "Levyi radikalizm, revoliutsionnyi demokratize i nauchyni sotsializm v stranakh Vostoka." *Rabochii klass i sovremennyi mir* no. 3 (1984):134–135.

Akhromeyev, Marshal S. F. "The Doctrine of Preventing War, Defending Peace and Socialism." *World Marxist Review* no. 12 (December 1987):23–28.

_____. *Voyenni entsiklopedicheskii slovar'*. Moscow: Voenizdat, 1986.

Alexander, Y., D. Carlton, and P. Wilkinson, eds. *Terrorism, Theory and Practice*. Boulder: Westview, 1979.

Andrianov, Col. V. "Partizanskaia voina i voennaia strategiia." *Voenno-istoricheskii zhurnal* no. 7 (1975):29–31.

Asoyan, Boris. "Time to Gather Stones Together." *International Affairs* no. 9 (1988):66–67.

_____. "Prisoner No. 220/82." *New Times* no. 51 (December 1987):12–13.

_____. "The Apartheid System Is Doomed." *International Affairs* no. 11 (1985):53–59.

Avyansky, Ze'ev. *Personal Terror [Hateror ha ishi]*. Tel Aviv: Kibbutz Hameuchad, 1977.

Bolotin, Boris. "Western Sahara – A Problem of Concern to the

World Community." *New Times* no. 39 (September 1988):9–12.

"The 'Breakthrough': A Joint Effort." *New Times* no. 19 (May 1988):12–15.

Brutents, Karen. *Sovremennye natsional'no-osvoboditelnye revoliutsii.* Moscow: Politizdat, 1974.

Chervov, Col. Gen. N. "Moguchii faktor mira." *Mezhdunarodnaia zhizn'* no. 2 (1988):10–18.

Clad, Thomas. "Betting on Violence." *Far Eastern Economic Review* (December 17, 1987):35–40.

Cline, Ray, and Yonah Alexander. *Terrorism: The Soviet Connection.* New York: Crane Russak, 1984.

Coker, Christopher. "Decolonization in the Seventies: Rhodesia and the Dialectic of National Liberation." *Round Table* no. 274 (1979):122–136.

Cooley, John. *Green March, Black September.* London: Frank Cass, 1973.

Day, John. "The Insignificance of Tribe in the African Politics of Zimbabwe-Rhodesia." *Journal of Commonwealth and Comparative Politics* 8, no. 1 (1980).

Dietl, Wilhelm. "Eastern Europe: The Quiet Business." In Aaron Karp, "Shades of Grey: The Hidden Arms Trade Today." Stockholm International Peace Research Institute, 1987, unpublished.

Dobrynin, Anatoly. "Soviet Foreign Policy: Basic Principles and New Thinking." *World Marxist Review* no. 3 (1988):15–28.

Dolgopolov, E. "Razoblachenie burzhuaznykh i maoistkikh fal'sifikatorov istorii lokal'nykh voin." *Voenno-istoricheskii zhurnal* no. 6 (1980):61–62.

Dolgopolov, Yevgeny. "Working for Independence: National Liberation Wars in a Nuclear Age." *Soviet Military Review* no. 7 (1987):50–51.

Dominguez-Reyes, Edme. "Soviet Academic Views on the Caribbean and Central America." Conference paper, International Association of Slavic Studies, Washington, D.C., 1985.

"Dvizhenie soprotivleniia rasistas usilivaetsia." *Mezhdunarodnaia zhizn'* no. 4 (1985):131 (Nzo interview).

Efimov, Major N. "Revoliutsionnyi protsess i sovremennost'." *Kommunist vooruzhennykh sil* no. 7 (1987):84–88.

Efremov, V. "Mezhdunarodnyi terroriza-orudie imperializma i reaktsii." *Aziia i Afrika segodnia* no. 7 (1981):24–26.

Elad, Shlomi, and Ariel Merari. *The Soviet Bloc and World Terrorism*. Tel Aviv: Jaffee Center for Strategic Studies, 1984.

Fedorov, Vladimir. "'Levyi' ekstremizm v politicheskoi zhizni stran Vostoka." *Aziia i Afrika segodnia* no. 5 (1983):13–16.

Freedman, Robert. "Soviet Policy towards International Terrorism," in Yonah Alexander, ed., *International Terrorism: National, Regional and Global Perspectives*. New York: Praeger, 1976.

Garthoff, Raymond. "New Thinking in Soviet Military Doctrine." *The Washington Quarterly* (Summer 1988):131–158.

Gerald-Scheepers, Thomas. "African Resistance in Rhodesia." *African Perspectives* no. 1 (1976):125–126.

Golan, Galia. *The Soviet Union and National Liberation Movements in the Third World*. London: Unwin and Hyman, 1988.

———. *The Soviet Union and the Palestine Liberation Organization: An Uneasy Alliance*. New York: Praeger, 1980.

Gorbachev, Mikhail. *Perestroika: New Thinking for Our Country and the World*. London: Collins, 1987.

Gorbunov, I. "Militarizatsiia obrechennogo rezhima," *Aziia i Afrika segodnia* no. 8 (1982):28–29.

Gordon, A. V. *Problemy natsional'no-osvoboditel'noi bor'by v tvorchestve Frantsa Fanona*. Moscow: Nauka, 1977.

Goren, Roberta. *The Soviet Union and Terrorism*. London: Allen and Unwin, 1984.

Grachev, Andrei. "The Boomerang of Terrorism." *New Times* no. 42 (1987):18–22.

Gromyko, Anatoly. "Neo-colonialism's Maneuvres in Southern Africa." *International Affairs* no. 12 (1977):98–99.

Gross, Feliks. *Violence in Politics*. The Hague: Mouton, 1972.

Haggani, Husain. "Pakistan: The Hands behind the Bomb." *Far Eastern Economic Review* (July 30, 1987):28–29.

———. "The Unseen Soviet Hand." *Far Eastern Economic Review* (October 29, 1987):44–45.

Hlanganani, Temba. "The Greatest Moment of My Life." *African Communist* no. 103 (1985):22–29.

Holloway, "The Red Army Returns." *Far Eastern Economic Review* (December 17, 1987):22–24.

Hough, Jerry. "The Evolving Soviet Debate on Latin America." *Latin American Research Review* 16, no. 1 (1981):131–132.

Iordanski, V. "The Policy of Neo-colonialism in Action." *International Affairs* no. 6 (1981):84.

Israeli, Raphael. *The PLO in Lebanon, Selected Documents*. London: Weidenfeld and Nicolson, 1983.

Izyumov, Alexei, and Andrei Kortunov. "The Soviet Union in the Changing World." *International Affairs* no. 8 (1988):46–56.

Jenkins, Brian. "International Terrorism: Choosing the Right Target." Santa Monica: Rand Paper, March 1981.

Katz, Mark. *The Third World in Soviet Military Thinking*. Baltimore: Johns Hopkins, 1982.

Kazakov, V. "Regional Conflicts and International Security." *International Affairs* no. 2 (1986):45–56.

Khazanov, A. M. "Angola: bor'ba za nezavisimost'." *Voprosy istorii* no. 8 (1978):118–119.

Khrobostov, Mikhail. "The Hard Road to a Settlement." *New Times* no. 33 (1988):8–9.

Kiva, A. "Great October and the National-Liberation Movement." *Aziia i Afrika segodnia* no. 11 (November 1987):6.

_____. "The Struggle against the Remnants of Colonialism and Neocolonialism." *International Affairs* no. 3 (1981):51–52.

Korshunov, Evgeny. "Who the Terrorists Are." *New Times* no. 14 (1986):11–12.

Kozyrev, Andrei. "Confidence and the Balance of Interests." *Mezhdunarodnaia zhizn'* no. 10 (1988):3–12.

Krylov, N. B., and I. A. Reshetov. "Gosudarstvennyi terrorizm – ugroza mezhdunarodnoi bezopasnosti." *Sovetsko gosudarstvo i pravo* no. 2 (1987):78–84.

Kudimov, Yuri. "ARENA Bids for Power." *New Times* no. 44 (1988):18–19.

Kuhne, Winrich. "A New Realism in Soviet-South African Relations?" *Stiftung Wissenschaft und Politik*, July 1988.

Kurz, Anat, ed. *Contemporary Trends in World Terrorism*. New York: Praeger, 1987.

Kurz, Anat, et al. *INTER 86: A Review of International Terrorism in 1986*. Jerusalem: Jaffee Center for Strategic Studies, 1986.

Laqueur, Walter. *The Age of Terrorism*. Boston: Little, Brown and Co., 1987.

"Latin America: Democracy Must Be Won, Not Waited For." *World Marxist Review* no. 7 (July 1988):88–100.

Leites, Nathan. *A Study of Bolshevism*. Glencoe, Ill.: Free Press, 1953.

Lenin, V. I. "Left-Wing Communism, an Infantile Disorder."

Collected Works. Vol. 31. Moscow: Progress Publishers, 1966.

Lobov, Col. Gen. Vladimir. "The Armed Forces and New Thinking." *New Times* no. 8 (1988):12–13.

Lodge, Tom. "The African National Congress in South Africa, 1967–1983: Guerrilla War and Armed Propaganda." *Journal of Contemporary African Studies* 3, no. 1/2, (1983–1984): 160.

Login, Col. Vasily. "The Revolution Must Defend Itself." *Soviet Military Review* no. 4 (April 1988):12–14.

Lytov, Col. B. "70th Anniversary of USSR Armed Forces." *Aviatsiya i kosmonavtika* no. 10 (October 1987):39–41.

Manchkha, P. I. *Aktual'nye problemy sovremennoi Afriki.* Moscow: Politizdat, 1979.

Martin, David, and Phyllis Johnson. *The Struggle for Zimbabwe.* London: Faber and Faber, 1981.

McDonald, Hamish. "Tangle over Tripoli." *Far Eastern Economic Review* (January 16, 1986):40.

――――. "New Caledonia: Kanak's French Leave." *Far Eastern Economic Review* (September 3, 1987):28–29.

Medvedko, Leonid. "A Time to Throw Stones and a Time to Collect Them." *New Times* no. 36 (1988):16–18.

Midtsev, Veniamin. "Of Terrorism or Its 'Godfathers'?" *New Times* no. 9 (1981):14–17.

Merari, Ariel, and Anat Kurz. *INTER: International Terrorism in 1987.* Jerusalem: Jaffee Center for Strategic Studies, 1988.

Mzala (South African journalist). "The Volcano of the People's Wrath." *World Marxist Review* no. 7 (July 1988):121–127.

Nel, Philip. "The Current Soviet Approach to South Africa and Its Implications." Unpublished paper, 1988.

――――. "The Earnestness of Being Unimportant: The Soviet Union and South Africa." *Soviet Review* 4, no. 6 (Nov.–Dec. 1988):7–10.

Nesuk, M. D. *Pro terrorizm.* L'viv: Kaminiar, 1986.

Nikitin, Maj. Gen. L., and Col. O. Ivanov. "Imperialism's Intrigues in the Near East." *Zarubezhnoye voyennoye obozreniye* no. 6 (June 1987):10–16.

"The Nineteenth All-Union CPSU Conference: Foreign Policy and Diplomacy." *International Affairs* no. 10 (1988):3–34.

Nosenko, Vladimir. "Sowing Fear Is Not a Way of Building Peace." *New Times* no. 12 (1989):9–11.

Ogarkov, Marshal Nikolai, ed. *Voyenni entsiklopedicheskii slovar'*. Moscow: Voenizdat, 1983.

Okulov, Vadim. "Nine Years and a Hundred Days." *New Times* no. 17 (1987):20–22.

Ovinnikov, Richard. "Glavnye slagsemye ustoichivogo mira." *Mezhdunarodnaia zhizn'* no. 5 (1988):10–19.

Papp, Daniel. "National Liberation during Detente: The Soviet Outlook." *International Journal* 32 (1976–1977):82–99.

Pavlov, V. "The Death of Prisoner No. 1066." *New Times* no. 20 (1981):10–11.

"Perestroika, the 19th Party Conference and Foreign Policy." *International Affairs* no. 7 (1988):3–40.

Petrovskii, Vladimir. "A New Concept of World Politics." *New Times* no. 14 (1988):5–7.

Pomeroy, William, ed. *Guerrilla Warfare and Marxism*. London: Lawrence and Wishart, 1969.

Porter, Gareth. "Philippine Communism after Marcos." *Problems of Communism* 36 (September–October 1987):14–35.

Possony, Stefan. *A Century of Conflict*. Chicago: Regenoy, 1953.

Primakov, E. M. *Vostok posle krakha kolonial'noi sistemy*. Moscow: Nauka, 1982.

_____. "Sovetskaia politika v regionalnikh konfliktakh." *Mezhdunarodnaia zhizn'* no. 5 (1988):3–9.

Prizel, Ilya. "Latin America: The Long March." *National Interest* no. 12 (Summer 1988):109–120.

Ra'anan, Uri, Robert Pfaltzgraff, Richard Shultz, Ernst Halperin, and Igor Lukes. *Hydra of Carnage*. Lexington, Mass.: Lexington Books, 1986.

Rasnitzyn, V. "The Apartheid Regime under Siege." *International Affairs* no. 10 (1985):118–120.

Serebryannikov, Lt. Gen. of Aviation V. "Sootnoshenie politicheskikh i voennykh sredstv v zashchite sotsializma." *Kommunist vooruzhennykh sil* no. 18 (September 1987):9–16.

Sergiyev, Artyon. "The Present Stage of the Non-Aligned Movement." *International Affairs* no. 12 (1986):106–113.

Shevardnadze, Eduard. "The 19th All-Union CPSU Conference: Foreign Policy and Diplomacy." *International Affairs* no. 10 (1988):12–19.

Shihepo, Aaron. "The Namibian Knot: A Bleeding Wound." *World Marxist Review* no. 4 (April 1988):121–125.

Shubin, V. "Fictions and Realities." *New Times* no. 50 (1985):13.

_____. "Mezhdu nakoval'nei i molotom." *Mezhdunarodnaia zhizn'* no. 3 (1985):36–37.

Sidorova, Galina. "Diplomacy and Glasnost." *New Times* no. 12 (1988):20.

Sobolev, A. I. "Leninskaia kontseptsiia mnogoobraziia putei sotsial'nogo razvitiia." *Voprosy istorii KPSS* no. 4 (1980):41–52.

Spitsyn, Sergei. "Passions Still Running High." *New Times* no. 42 (1988):10–11.

Sovetskaia voennaia entsiklopediia. Vol. 8. Moscow: Voenizdat, 1980.

Stability and Security — A Common Concern. Moscow: Novosti, 1986.

Sterling, Claire. *The Terror Network.* New York: Berkley Books, 1981.

Tambo, Oliver. "Rumbling Volcano." *New Times* no. 38 (1985):26–27.

Tarabrin, Evgeny. "Peking's Maneuvres in Africa." *New Times* no. 6 (1972):18–19.

Tasker, Rodney. "Trouble from the South." *Far Eastern Economic Review* (May 21, 1987):46–47.

Terekhov, Vladimir. "International Terrorism and the Fight against It." *New Times* no. 11 (1974):20–21.

Tetiokin, V. "Real'nosti protivoborstva." *Aziia i Afrika segodnia* no. 11 (1987):26–28.

"The USSR and the Third World." *International Affairs* no. 12 (1988):134–145.

Tiagunenko, V. L., et al. *Vooruzhennaia bor'ba narodov Afriki za svobodu i nezavisimost'.* Ministerstvo Oborony-SSSR. Moscow: Nauka, 1974.

Titov, I. "Northern Ireland: Ten Years of Repression." *New Times* no. 51 (1982):22–23.

Tolz, Vera. "Soviet Press Treatment of Terrorism." Radio Free Europe-Radio Liberty, RL 161/86 (April 17, 1986):1–6.

Turkatenko, N. D. "Raschety i proschety Vashingtona v Iuzhoi Afrike." *SShA: ekonomika, politika, ideologiia* no. 2 (1977): 24–35.

Urban, Joan Barth. "Contemporary Soviet Perspectives on Revolution in the West." *Orbis* 19, no. 4 (1976):1359–1402.

Urnov, Andrei. "The Windhoek Farce." *New Times* no. 29 (1985): 22.

U.S. Department of State. *Patterns of Global Terrorism: 1986.* Washington, D.C., January 1988.

_____. *Patterns of Global Terrorism: 1987.* Washington, D.C., August 1988.

U.S. House of Representatives. Committee on Internal Security. *Terrorism.* Staff Study. Washington, D.C.: Government Printing Office, 1974.

Uzhegov, Col. Timofei (ret.), and Maj. Sergei Menyailo. "Partisan Warfare." *Soviet Military Review* no. 5 (May 1988):42–44.

Vinogradov, Yuri. "Conflict in Sri Lanka." *International Affairs* no. 4 (1988):68–73.

Vitaliev, K. "Imperialist Policy and the Conflict in South Africa." *International Affairs* no. 11 (1982):43–50.

Vitiuk, Viktor. *Leftist Terrorism.* Moscow: Progress Publishers, 1984.

_____. *Pod chuzhimi snamenami.* Moscow: Mysl, 1985.

Volkogonov, Col. Gen. Dmitry. "The Anti-War Doctrine." *New Times* no. 25 (June 1987):14–15.

Volkogonov, Lt. Gen. D. "Chelovecheskii faktor: puti adtivizatsii." *Kommunist vooruzhennykh sil* no. 2 (January 1987):9–18.

"The Way of the Anti-Imperialist Struggle in Tropical Africa." *World Marxist Review* no. 8 (1971):30–34.

Wolfowitz, Paul. "Southeast Asia: Deferring Hard Choices." *National Interest* no. 12 (Summer 1988):128–129.

Yazov, General D. T. *Na strazhe sotsializma i mira.* Moscow: Voenizdat, 1987.

Yefimov, Maj. Nikolai. "The Calculations and Miscalculations of the 'New Crusaders.'" *Soviet Military Review* no. 8 (August 1986):50–52.

Yodfat, Aryeh. "The USSR and the Palestinians." *New Outlook* no. 19 (1976):30–33.

Zgersky, Dmitry. "Yasser Arafat in Moscow." *New Times* no. 16 (April 1988):9.

Zhitomirsky, Vladimir. "Cold-Blooded Murder." *New Times* no. 36 (1981):10–11.

_____. "People and Bullets." *New Times* no. 32 (August 1988):17–19 and no. 16 (April 1988):13–16.

_____. "N. Ireland Tension." *New Times* no. 18 (May 1981):15.

Zhukov, Y., L. Delyusin, A. Iskenderov, and L. Stepanov. *The Third World.* Moscow: Progress Publishers, 1970.

Index